Anonymous

A Review of the Principles and Conduct of the Judges of His Majesty's Supreme Court of Judicature in Bengal

Or, an enguiry into the causes that have obstructed or defeated the salutary ends proposed by the legislature in establishing this court ..

Anonymous

A Review of the Principles and Conduct of the Judges of His Majesty's Supreme Court of Judicature in Bengal
Or, an enguiry into the causes that have obstructed or defeated the salutary ends proposed by the legislature in establishing this court ..

ISBN/EAN: 9783337312541

Printed in Europe, USA, Canada, Australia, Japan

Cover: Foto ©Suzi / pixelio.de

More available books at **www.hansebooks.com**

A

REVIEW

OF THE

PRINCIPLES AND CONDUCT

OF THE

JUDGES of his Majesty's Supreme Court
of Judicature in BENGAL.

A REVIEW

OF THE

PRINCIPLES AND CONDUCT

OF THE

JUDGES of His Majesty's Supreme Court of Judicature in BENGAL:

OR,

AN ENQUIRY

INTO THE

CAUSES that have obstructed or defeated the salutary ENDS proposed by the Legislature in establishing this COURT.

The best of human Institutions answer their end in part only, and from the first, and whilst the impression of the force that set them a going, lasts; and never fail to slacken afterwards, or to take new impressions from contingent events, by which they degenerate, and insensibly become NEW INSTITUTIONS under old Names.   BOLINGBR.

Printed in the year MDCCLXXXII.

PREFACE.

ANY attempt to throw new light upon a Subject that has been so much canvassed, as the Administration of Justice in Bengal, will probably be ridiculed as the effort of vanity and presumption. That the Natives of India should be upheld and protected " in the " enjoyment of their antient laws, usages, " rights, and privileges*," is a position so consonant to humanity and sound policy, that, late as it has been received into our Statute-book, it ought always to have regulated our counsels. I have not indulged a gaudy display of argument, in order to establish this position, which, in my opinion, the shortest Chapter in Montesquieu would be long enough to prove. It is the application of a Principle clear in itself, but difficult to be accommodated to our situation in Bengal, where the mixt body of British Subjects and Natives form the joint object of Legislation, that is alone to be considered.

The generous hope of protecting the Natives, by sending them our laws, and of trans-

---

* Vide Preamble to the temporary Act passed last year, 21 Geo. III, c. 70.

fusing

fusing into their breasts a manly confidence in an equal dispensation of Justice, has certainly not answered in the event; and while we fondly imagined we had given them to drink " of " the pure fountain of British Liberty," the draught has been poisoned by the hands that administered it.

Seven years have elapsed since our Lawyers and our Laws were transported to Bengal. At the expiration of this term, the business of Legislation is now to be begun afresh. We have heard from the Throne a solemn recommendation to Parliament*, *to consider the state and condition of the British possessions in the East Indies, and by what means the happiness of the native Inhabitants may be best promoted.*

In so important a subject, the lowest understanding may furnish valuable hints. In so extensive a work, the meanest labourer may be of use. To consider by what means the happiness of the Natives may be best promoted, it is first necessary to point out by what means it has been chiefly obstructed. This, as far as respects the Administration of Justice in Bengal, is the object of the present Inquiry, which is

* His Majesty's Speech at the commencement of the present Session.

humbly

humbly offered to the attention of those who are able, by their station and talents, to apply a remedy to the mischiefs that have been experienced.

The Facts that are here brought forward, are neither susceptible of ornament nor exaggeration. In stating them I have paid no attention to the profound conjectures of those *candid* persons, who suppose the Complaints that have been sent from India are only the offspring of Clamour, or the machinations of British Subjects abroad, desirous of shaking off the restraints of law. This compendious Answer, to facts that cannot be denied, and to inferences from facts that cannot be resisted, may be flattering to the prejudices of some, and afford a ready and prompt excuse for the laziness of others, in declining the examination of an intricate subject, where there is nothing to gratify vanity, interest, or ambition.—As I would not, however, unadvisedly offend against any man's prejudices *,

which

* I am not fond of accusing the *prejudices* of others, as I question whether a prejudiced person was ever cured by being told that he was so; and at best it is an oblique mode of begging the question. According to all parties, Prejudice has had so much to do, and Reason so little,

which it might be in my power to remove, I have generally taken the authority of the Judges for the facts themselves, where-ever they are not contradicted by stronger proofs. The Declarations and Letters of the Chief Justice, and the other Judges, that appear printed in the Report of the Select Committee of last year, have not been hitherto sufficiently noticed. I consider the comparison of those Letters, at different periods, as affording the most decisive interpretation of their Conduct. If the result is not favourable to their Cause, they must abide by the maxim of law—*Verba accipiuntur fortiùs contra proferentes.*

little, in this whole subject, that I am heartily tired of the word. The British Subjects say, it was *prejudice* against them that first sent out a Court of Judicature, with inquisitorial Powers, to Bengal. The Judges say, that *prejudice* against the Lawyers has given birth to the complaints of their having extended the Jurisdiction of the Court over the Natives, and has made them so unpopular both in India and Europe:—and the British Subjects reply, that nothing but *prejudice* can make this defence of the violent and injudicious conduct of the Judges be received in England. It is well known, the *prejudices* of the natives have prevented our laws from being favourably received among them; and it is probable that the *prejudices* of our Lawyers, to the forms of their profession, have in their turn increased the Prejudices of the Natives. Thus we see PREJUDICES dancing in a circle, and reciprocally displayed as cause and effect of each other, to the end of the Chapter.

The

PREFACE. ix

The representations of the Governor and Council of Bengal (to which I have often occasion to refer) are not, I confess, the most unexceptionable Evidence to affect the Judges. At one time they were Parties against the Supreme Court in the strongest sense; insomuch that the Chief Justice charges them with using every effort, and employing the most disingenuous arts to undermine the Court by secret influence, and oppose it by open hostility*. But as the Chief Justice himself soon afterwards accepted a Post under the Governor and Council, revocable at their pleasure, and immediately under their controul, this objection appears to me to be done away. They are no longer to be considered as opposing parties; they are restored to their competency as witnesses; and the Chief Justice cannot except to the Evidence of those in whose hands (notwithstanding his former insinuations) he has chosen to confide his fortune and honour.

If this be a hard rule of evidence, its effect can only be taken off by a supposition, not very honourable to the contending parties, viz. that their reciprocal accusations were only fitted to answer temporary purposes; that they have written to England, not what they knew to be true,

* Sir Elijah Impey's Letters to his Majesty's Principal Secretary of State. Dated March 2, 1780.

but

but what they wiſhed to be believed; and have conſidered words " as the counters of wiſe " men, and the money of fools," which if the good people of England were willing to take without weighing, they anſwered juſt as well. But as this ſuſpicion would introduce a general ſcepticiſm upon a ſubject that requires the ſpeedy deciſion of the Legiſlature, and would equally ſuſpend our aſſent to the repreſentations of both parties, I had rather impute any exaggerations that may occur to the natural warmth of argument. This is an indulgence which, while I allow it to others, I ought to claim for myſelf, if I ſhall appear to have been betrayed into any improper aſperity of language on the conduct of the Profeſſors of our law at Calcutta.—Laudable as it is, in general (ſays a popular Writer), to keep one's temper, there are certain occaſions when it is even laudable to loſe it;—and I own I cannot contemplate, with calmneſs, the confuſion and miſery that has ariſen from the introduction of our laws into Bengal; and the perverſion of a noble Syſtem of Juriſprudence, which in this country is our Security and our Glory!!

March 18, 1782.

CONTENTS.

OCCASION of establishing a Supreme Court of Judicature in Bengal, page 1--9. Reason for including natives of a certain description within its jurisdiction, p. 10. Want of precision in describing the objects of this jurisdiction, p. 11, 12. Observations on the constitution of the Court, and the powers with which it was invested, p. 12—25. Importance and delicacy of the trust reposed in the JUDGES; and difficulty of applying the laws of England to a Distant People, p. 29—31. Appointment of a Governor-General and Council, p. 32. Powers of the Court and Council co-ordinate, and no third power to mediate in case of Collision, p. 33—36. Dissensions between the Members of the Council, p. 37. The Judges take a part in these dissensions, and considered very early as political Judges, p. 39. Extension of their power and influence in the settlement, along with the extension of their jurisdiction, p. 43—60. Collision with the Provincial Court of Judicature, and Imprisonment of the Mahomedan Lawyers, the Cauzee, and Muftees of the Patna Court, p. 65—73. Attempt made to extend the Jurisdiction over the ZEMINDARS of Bengal, in the case of the RAJAH of Cossijurah, p. 75. The Governor and Council interpose to protect the Zemindar by a military force, p. 77.

Violent

CONTENTS.

Violent proceedings of the Judges in vindication of their authority; several persons imprisoned for Contempt of the Court; and denunciations of the like punishment held out in terrorem *to all British Subjects, who should be aiding and assisting the Governor and Council, p. 78—82. The Governor and Council transmit a petition to Parliament for an Act of Indemnity for having resisted the Court, p. 84—85. Sudden* COMPROMISE *between the Governor and the Chief Justice; the latter appointed Judge of the Sudder Adaulut with a salary of 8000 l. per Annum, p. 86—93. Nature of this appointment, and observations, p. 93—101, et seq. Assent or dissent of the other Judges, p. 118 (Notes). Summary observations on the Conduct of the Judges, and of the Chief Justice in particular; and on the tendency and effects of this appointment, 119. et seq. Conclusion, recommending either a new modification of the Supreme Court, or its absolute removal. 141, et seq. Doubts as to the operation of the temporary Act that passed last year. Happiness of the natives how best consulted.*

A REVIEW

OF THE

Principles and Conduct of the Judges of his Majesty's Supreme Court of Judicature in Bengal, &c.

INTRODUCTION.

IT shall be my endeavour, in the following pages, to explain, in as clear and as intelligible a manner as I am able, the nature and foundation of those complaints, concerning the extension of the laws of England to the natives of Bengal, which have for so long a time resounded in the public ear; while it is to be apprehended that few, if any, distinct images have been conveyed to the understanding. The indignation of every liberal mind, at the idea of imposing a complicated system of laws upon a people, no less averse to our institutions, than invincibly attached to their own; concurring with a general difguft at the conduct of a rapacious herd of lawyers, who fought their own aggrandifement in pulling down the ancient ufages of the country, carried the opponents of the Court of Judicature to a degree of warmth on this fubject, that could hardly be blamed even in its excefs.

It has been often obferved, that in fome queftions men's feelings run before their underftandings, even where they both terminate in the fame point. The warmth and zeal that prevailed laft year on this fubject, may be fuppofed to be now confiderably abated, either by the natural effect of fatiated curiofity, or by the acceffion of new fubjects of more preffing importance. I think it may therefore be of fervice to the Public, to give an account of the rife and progrefs of this novel Judicature in Bengal, that the true ftate of the difpute may not flide from memory, and that men, who have been conducted right by their feelings, may not be led wrong in their reafonings.

It may hereafter be the object of much curious inveftigation; and, in a century or two, when the name of the Supreme Court will be forgotten, when our laws and our lawyers are extirpated from Bengal, and when the Britifh Power itfelf is fwept away from the face of that country,

country, it will probably, I fay, become an object of much curious fpeculation to fome enquiring philofopher (fome future writer *de l'Efprit des Loix*), to obferve in what manner, and with what fuccefs, a free and enlightened people attempted to communicate their laws to the conquered provinces of the Eaft, and with what felection of its general principles, and with what dereliction of its technical rules and municipal conftitution, this attempt was made. The enquiry will be inftructive.— I wifh it were likely to end in a high admiration either of our laws or its profeffors—but I believe future times will hardly clafs Sir Elijah Impey* with either Solon or Juftinian.

In the prefent difcuffion, I fhall proceed with an Englifhman's veneration for the laws of his country, and at the fame time fhall endeavour to preferve a philofophic regard for the rights of mankind, however diftant in place, or differing in colour.

It is not neceffary, at this time, to recur to thofe periods in which the United Eaft-India Company (a body of Merchants bearing a very trifling proportion, either in number or in wealth, to the Merchants of Great Britain at large) acquired the territorial poffeffions of

---

* Chief Juftice of the Supreme Court.

three

three of the richest provinces in the Mogul's Empire, and instead of mixing in the intrigues, and depending on the precarious friendship of the Viceroys (or Nabobs) of the Empire, thought it necessary to take the cards into their own hands, and to play the game themselves. These are matters I leave to more voluminous writers. It is sufficient to say, that the Company became, in virtue of the treaty of 1765, possessed of the territorial revenues and possessions of Bengal, Bahar, and Orissa, subject however to its antient laws, and subject to those common implied compacts by which mankind were first cemented in society; namely, that they should pursue the happiness of their subjects:—a compact by the way too likely to escape the memory and attention of Merchants, whose general object is commerce and not glory, and to whom *profit and loss* is the polar star by which they are directed in their course.

The important trust of governing these great and newly-acquired dominions were, *ex necessitate*, committed to the Company's Servants who were upon the spot; many of whom were rash and inconsiderate, and some of them were profligate and mercenary. In the confusion always attendant upon great changes and revolutions, no doubt some enormities were committed; at the same time it ought to be allowed,

lowed, that great abilities, and great virtues too, were difplayed by others of the Company's Servants*, who maintained their integrity; abilities and virtues which their fituation alone, and the great fcenes in which they acted, feem to have formed or called forth.—Without an education in the fchool of politics, they difcovered, on many occafions, the greateft political knowledge.—With few literary advantages, their writings are often highly eloquent; and when the torrent of abufe that has been poured upon our countrymen in India has fubfided, the Public will remember with gratitude the names of Vanfittart and of many others, who will have that juftice done to their memory which was refufed them when living.

To return to the period I have been fpeaking of.—Had an Englifh Court of Judicature (with fuch immenfe powers as the Supreme Court at prefent poffeffes) then exifted in India, it might have been of real utility in checking the fpirit of rapacity and intrigue at that unfet-

* " Let the Servants of the Company have the merit
" they are entitled to. The Court of Directors furely
" will not claim to themfelves the merit of thofe advan-
" tages, which the Nation and the Company are at pre-
" fent in poffeffion of. The officers of the Navy and
" Army have had great fhare in the execution; but the
" Company's Servants were the Cabinet Council who
" planned every thing; and to them alfo may be afcribed
" fome part of the merit of our great acquifitions." Parliamentary Debates, A. D. 1772.

tled period between the diffolution of the Nabob's power and the eftablifhment of the Englifh government; that fort of *twilight* (as Mr. Burke expreffively called it), under the fhelter of which bad men were guilty of great abufes: but, like almoft all the legiflative acts of Britain (never ready with its well-planned projects till the time of employing them is paft), a Court of Judicature was not fent out for this falutary purpofe till feveral years afterwards; when our Government there had affumed a fettled form; when regulations had been framed to prevent a return of the fame abufes, and when the face of the country (like the face of nature after a ftorm is over-blown) became once more quiet, tranquil, and comparatively happy. Long before the Judges arrived, new and important reformations had actually taken effect. Councils of Revenue were eftablifhed in the different provinces; the ableft of the Company's Servants, and men of the faireft characters in the Settlement, were felected to prefide jointly in matters of revenue; and each in rotation, affifted by the *Cauzees* and *Muftees* (the antient eftablifhed Magiftrates of the country), appointed to difpenfe juftice to the natives. Mr. Haftings, who was at that time Prefident, and whofe abilities are generally admitted, drew up a fet of Regulations for thefe two important departments. The Regulations for the Adminiftration of Juftice were very juftly applauded by Sir E. Impey on his arrival in that country. He has fince changed his opinion: he now only calls them *fpecious*; and fays, that however excellent they may appear in theory, they have never been ftrictly adhered to in practice.

While thefe Regulations were framing in Bengal, the fubject was taken up with great warmth and vigour in Parliament. The men who had been active in the firft fcenes of plunder and peculation, were returned from India. The fplendor of their equipages, and the profufion of their expences, dazzled and difgufted the old eftablifhed gentry of this country, who had much better blood flowing in their veins than thefe *upftart Nabobs*, as they were contemptuoufly ftiled. Nothing was talked of for a whole Seffion of Parliament but ftories of Indian rapacity. Imaginary Nabobs who never exifted, and real Nabobs who were ftill living, were faid to have been cruelly murdered for the fake of their wealth; and Credulity, with open mouth, fwallowed all that exaggeration could amplify, or artifice invent. An immenfe majority of that Houfe of Commons, who afterwards voted, without a blufh, for the raifing a revenue in America, for the fole purpofe of fhifting their own expences on the Americans, and (on finding themfelves refifted in their object) proceeded to enforce the demand by lay-ing waste the Colonies with fire and sword, and plunging them into all the aggravated horrors of war; that very House of Commons affected to contemplate, with pious detestation, the large fortunes obtained in India by their countrymen; by many of them after long and meritorious services to the Company, and by most of them after a long residence in an unwholesome climate, from which one in twenty never returns.

In saying this, I would not be thought to extenuate the abuses committed in India, and much less to excuse one charge of rapacity by another. Those abuses certainly did exist in a great degree; and the measure of sending out a Court of Judicature, to punish or prevent them in future; was highly proper, if it had been done in a proper temper.

To proceed.—A Court of Judicature was to be erected with all possible speed; and four Barristers of small practice (but of great spirit and undoubted integrity) were forthwith exalted into Judges. Having equipped themselves with large wigs and venerable robes, and being furnished with *Viner's Abridgment of the Laws of England*, in 22 vols. folio, *The Attorney's Practice in the King's Bench and Common Pleas*, in 4 vols. octavo, and *John Doe* and *Richard Roe* as supporters, they set sail, in the memorable year of our Lord 1774, to preach

preach the *good tidings* of Redress to the Gentoos and Mahometans, and to denounce punishment and castigation on their European oppressors. Such was the object of this new *mission*, as Sir E. Impey gravely calls it.

Every power that could be conceived necessary to this end, was lavished upon the Court and its Judges.—They were armed with the founding title of his Majesty's *Supreme Court of Judicature* *; they were invested with Civil Law, Common Law, Ecclesiastical, Admiralty, and Criminal Jurisdiction ; they were to try Europeans on personal actions, and to assess damages without a Jury † ; they were to punish them with whipping ‡ and the pillory, if they shewed a contempt of the Court by disobeying its subpœnas ;

* This was *pro majori dignitate*. The Reader is not to infer from the name (as some have done) that they were a Court of Appeal from the native Courts of Justice ; they had no legal interference with them.

† To compass the laudable objects of this Institution, here was a violent breach made in the Law of England, which declares that no Englishman shall suffer in his property or his person without the verdict of twelve men, who are his equals. *Nisi per judicium parium, aut per legem terræ.*

‡ In the late heats and dissentions at Calcutta, the Chief Justice so far forgot himself, and that propriety we are accustomed to see and admire in our English Judges, as to declare from the Bench, " that the clause in the King's
" Letters-

pœnas; and lastly, to prevent them from eluding justice, under colour of employing the natives in the commission of their crimes, " EVERY native, directly or indirectly in their " Service, or in that of the Company," was to be made subject to the jurisdiction of this Court likewise.

———Hinc illæ lacrymæ———
———Hæc prima mali labes *.

This

" Letters-patent was inserted at *his own* express desire."— Mr. Hickey's Evidence.—Report of the Select Committee of the House of Commons, page 71.

Such a declaration from a Judge on the Bench, that *he* suggested a clause impowering him to *whip or pillory* the inhabitants of a British Settlement, gave the persons who heard it no very favourable impression of that same Judge's moderation and impartiality, who was appointed to try causes, and assess damages against them, without the intervention of a Jury!

" Miserable indeed" (they observed in strong and pointed terms of indignation) " must be the situation of Britons, " to be under the weight of such Powers, with such an " interpreter!"—Vide printed Remarks on their Petition to Parliament.

* By an unfortunate want of precision in the Statute, and in the King's Letters-patent appointing the Supreme Court, the Judges were empowered to hear, not only complaints of oppression against natives within the above description, but *all* suits whatever; in consequence of which the English laws, in their full extent, were let in at once upon these ignorant natives, and " from this one source" (as an ingenious Writer has expressed it) " have diffused them-
" selves

This anxiety to comprehend all natives, who might be made the inſtruments of oppreſſion by the Engliſh Gentlemen, introduced thoſe vague and undefined words,—*all perſons, directly or indirectly, in the ſervice of the ſaid United Eaſt-India Company, or any of his Majeſty's ſubjects* †. Here was the door left open for that latitude of interpretation, which, to the infinite emolument of the attornies, has extended this juriſdiction over every native whom it has been thought worth while to bring within it. Here was the ſeminal principle, the " grain of muſtard-ſeed ‡," which, by means of the foſtering care of the Judges of the Court, and the unceaſing dexterity of its Practiſers, has been expanded to its preſent ſize; and by drawing along with it the immenſe body of our

" ſelves by innumerable channels over the whole country, " and pervaded every connection of life, public and pri-" vate, domeſtic and ſocial." Obſervations on the Adminiſtration of Juſtice in Bengal, 4to.—The confuſion that this muſt occaſion in *any* country, and much more in Bengal, may be eaſily conceived!

† 13 Geo. III. cap. 63. § 14.

‡ St. Matth. chap. xiii. ver. 30, 31. " Like unto a " grain of muſtard-ſeed, which a man took and ſowed in " his field, which indeed is *the leaſt of all ſeeds*, but when " it is grown it is the greateſt among herbs, and becometh " a tree, ſo that the birds of the air come and lodge in the " branches thereof."—The Attornies of the Supreme Court are " the birds of the air" who have lodged in the branches of this new Juriſdiction.

laws,

laws, with all its rules, fictions, and inapplicable forms, has, in effect, converted the edge of this new Court of Judicature *against* the natives, for whose benefit and security it was intended.—" To work effects contrary to their
" intention (says an eloquent Writer), is a
" fate that too often attends the best of human
" expedients; and the reflection does no ho-
" nour to our wisdom or our foresight."

Before I venture further into the detail, the Reader must indulge me with a few observations on the Structure and Constitution of this Court of Judicature. Out of the many that crowd upon my mind, the following seem to me of importance.

I. I shall observe that the Supreme Court was invested with a *twofold* jurisdiction; one local, that is, confined within the limits of the British factory; the other personal, or extending to persons falling under a certain character or description. This idea of giving the same Court, and the same Judges, a double jurisdiction, was declared by a great and truly respectable man [*], at the head of the House of Peers, to be a *novel* experiment; and I hope to God we shall see no more such experiments!

[*] Lord Thurlow.

The

The Reader will easily perceive the difference between the two sorts of jurisdiction*.
The

* The city of London, the Counties Palatine of Lancaster, &c. &c. are instances of a *local* jurisdiction. The Court of Exchequer, on the other hand, exercises a *personal* jurisdiction, that is, over the King's debtors and accountants; and its jurisdiction accordingly soon became universal: for the Court allows a suitor to bring an action against any person whatever, and on suggesting that he (the plaintiff) is a debtor of the King's, and that unless the party complained of be made to pay his demand, he shall be less able to satisfy the King's debt, the Process of the Court issues, which is called a Quo minus (from these *words, Quo minus sufficiens existit,* to pay the King's debt). Now all this is mere *fiction* of law; and such fictions are, among Lawyers, held highly meritorious. Mr. Justice Le Maistre, soon after the Supreme Court arrived in India, was imprudent enough to declare, that he would engage to bring every native of Bengal within its jurisdiction, by a slight variation in the form of a common writ of *Capias*.

The King's Bench has obtained a similar jurisdiction in civil actions, on *suggesting* that the defendant had been guilty of a breach of the peace (which is never allowed to be controverted), and then the defendant is chargeable in any other action.

Both these jurisdictions are in fact usurpations upon the Court of Common Pleas; but as the law of the land is the rule of all the three Courts, no inconvenience is felt by the subject; and, on the contrary, a beneficial emulation is excited between the different Judges, who shall most facilitate justice.

But is it so in Bengal? Can it be indifferent to the native whether he is tried by the laws of his own country, or the laws of England? By his native Magistrates, or by foreign

The limits of place are tolerably fixed; and nothing short of an earthquake or an inundation can shift them. But where the question turns upon the construction, of what persons fall within such and such a verbal definition, the distinctions are infinite; and are in fact as endless as metaphysical sophistry, combined with legal quibbles, can make them. A Chief Justice, in his definition of the one, is confined by metes and land-marks; in the other, he is the arbiter of his own jurisdiction, and may compress or relax it at pleasure.

II. If it was the sole intention of the legislature (as I solemnly believe it was) to fence the feeble Indian against the oppression and rapacity of Europeans, and likewise of his own countrymen, when acting under the immediate influence of Europeans, the powers of the Court should have been confined (as has been already hinted) to the single point of rapine and oppression. The means should have been commensurate to the end, and no more than commensurate. The Reader will hear with surprise, and perhaps with indignation, that for one action brought by native against na-

reign Judges? By a simple form of Judicature, or by a complicated system of positive laws, of which he has not the smallest acquaintance till he finds this knowledge in his sufferings?

tive,

tive, for offences of the fort the Legiflature had in view, fifty are tried in queftions of Meum and Tuum, and other private rights, where the laws of England ought never to have been interpofed.

III. This objection applies, in a ftill ftronger manner, to the criminal laws of England. The Company fucceeding to the power and place of the ancient Sovereigns of the country, it was natural for the natives of high rank and dignity to wifh to retain the appearance of their ancient confequence, by connecting themfelves with the Company in the executive departments of their new Government. It was equally politic and neceffary for the Company to encourage this difpofition, and to leave certain high offices in the hands of the natives, as well as the poffeffions of their ancient diftricts, referving the accuftomed revenues. But little did the natives imagine they thereby* became fubject to all the voluminous laws of England; or that, in acting under the eftablifhed laws and ufages of their native country, they were to have their actions tried by a different ftandard, againft which they could not poffibly fufpect they had offended;

* As coming under the defcription of the Statute, of " INDIRECTLY in the Service of the Company."—What, by paying a quit-rent or a revenue for large territorial jurifdictions! Even fo.

and

and even their lives brought in jeopardy on any one of our numerous Statutes, the long catalogue of whose capital felonies (amounting I think to upwards of ONE HUNDRED AND SIXTY-FOUR) has long been a disgrace to our national humanity, if the extreme mildness of the Prerogative did not so frequently step in between the criminal and the laws.

I shall not here revive the question of Nundecomar, a Gentoo of great rank and opulence, who was executed, in 1775, on the Statute of Geo. II. for a forgery committed nine years before the Court was established. Peace be to his ashes! The dangerous intriguing spirit of that great and daring man might make it allowable to hunt him out of society, *per fas atque nefas*; but as I take it to be an old and a just rule, that 'the State ought ' never to countenance such proceedings against ' the worst and most guilty of men, as may be ' applied to destroy the best and most innocent;' so I cannot help considering this whole transaction is a stain upon our English jurisprudence. Any obnoxious native, possessing high power, may, according to that precedent, be *taken off*, if an obsolete English Statute can be discovered, to which he has made himself unwittingly liable; and an arrow drawn from the same quiver of our Statute-felonies, might slay the *Subahdar* of Bengal, or the GRAND MOGUL

Mogul * himself, if he should ever venture within the limits of this new-fangled constructive jurisdiction.

* The Grand Mogul receives a pension from the Company. I confess the reasoning of the Court of Directors, on the case of Nundecomar, appears to my mind irresistibly strong. In a Memorial they presented to his Majesty's Secretary of State in 1777, is the following passage: "We beg your Lordship to consider what will be the con-
"sequences, if the Judges proceed upon the principle of
"declaring all the other parts of the criminal law of Eng-
"land to be in force in Bengal; and they must so pro-
"ceed, if they mean to be consistent with themselves.
"Can it be just or prudent to introduce all the different
"species of felony created by that which is called the
"*Black Act*? Or to involve, as what is called the *Co-
"ventry Act* involves, offences of different degrees in one
"common punishment? Or to introduce the endless, and
"almost inexplicable distinctions, by which certain acts
"are or are not burglary? Can certain offenders be tran-
"sported to his Majesty's Colonies in America, or sent to
"work upon the river Thames? Shall every man, con-
"victed for the first time of bigamy, which is allowed,
"protected, nay almost commanded by their law, be
"burnt in the hand if he can read, and hanged if he
"cannot read?—These, my Lord, are some only of the
"consequences which we conceive must follow, if the cri-
"minal law of England be suffered to remain in force,
"and binding upon the natives of Bengal. If it were
"legal to try, to convict, and execute *Nundecomar* for for-
"gery, on the Statute of George II. it must, as we con-
"ceive, be equally legal to try, convict, and to punish the
"*Subahdar* of *Bengal*, and all his Court, for bigamy, upon
"the Statute of *James* I."—Vide Report of the Committee of the House of Commons, Appendix, No. 2.

IV. A limited power, over natives of a certain description, was given the Supreme Court on the following principle; the *equity* and legality of which (however plausible) I never could thoroughly understand. It was supposed, that if Europeans only were subject, they would exert their influence over the natives in their service, to exercise oppressions which they themselves would fear to commit, and by this stratagem escape with impunity. Now I confess that the idea of the European eluding punishment, and letting the vengeance of the Court fall only upon the ignorant servile native, who probably durst not disobey the commands of his superior, seems to me a strange instance of legislative wisdom. If considered with a reference to fact, it is cruel and unjust; if as a declaration of law, it was illegal; for no British subject could screen himself by employing a native: the well-known maxim *qui facit per alium facit per se,* would be an insuperable bar to the excuse.

V. A solemn judgment of the Court of Common Pleas, pronounced only three years after this new Court was erected *, is a decided confirmation that the whole system proceeded

---

* Blackstone's Reports, lately published, 2d Vol. Case of Rafael against Verelst.

upon an erroneous opinion of the law of the land; for there Sir William De Grey, Sir William Blackstone, and the other venerable Judges of that Court, expressly declared, in the case of an action against Mr. Verelst, late Governor of Bengal, that the Governor was liable to an action of trespass, for having by letter commanded, or at least influenced, SUJAH DOWLAH, the *Nabob* of *Oude*, to imprison the plaintiff, who was an Armenian merchant. Lord Chief Justice De Grey expressly says, " I consider the Nabob as not being actor in this case, but the act to be done in point of law, by those who procured or commanded it; and in them it may doubtless be a trespass. *Sujah Dowlah* was a mere instrument. He acted not from any motives of his own, but gave way through awe or fear."—It happened, indeed, that *Sujah Dowlah* was not amenable to the English laws; but in the case of a common native of Bengal, if he should " give way through awe and fear," is the whole weight of the English laws to fall upon the ignorant native, while the British subject escapes? Yet such is the humane, liberal, and sagacious plan, on which the Supreme Court of Judicature exercises jurisdiction over the miserable natives within its circle.

VI. There was indeed another reason that influenced the Legislature to include certain natives within the jurisdiction, which was, that before the Company took the Government of Bengal into their own hands, before they became Sovereigns, and while they were contented to be merchants (though even then they possessed immense power and influence in the country), they enjoyed, among other advantages, a right of trading DUTY FREE in the *Nabob*'s dominions; and this right their Servants under them likewise claimed and exercised. It is well known, that certain native merchants, under the name of *Banyans* or *Gomastahs**, were accustomed to furnish the younger Servants of the Company, who were commonly extravagant and needy, with large sums of money, in order to insinuate themselves into their confidence; and under cover of their protection, and in their names, to exercise this lucrative privilege of trading *Duty-free*. These Banyans committed great abuses, and were said to have been guilty of great extortion under this cover: and it was for the purpose of meeting and overthrowing these practices, that natives, " directly or indi-
" rectly, in the Service of British Subjects, or
" the Company, were included within the juris-

---

* Stewards or Agents.   " diction."

" diction."—But it seems to have been forgotten, at the time the Act passed, that the Company's situation was almost wholly altered within a few years; that, instead of claiming an exemption from the Nabob's Duties and Customs, they themselves became the Sovereigns of the country; that this claim of privilege was absorbed in their new relation, and was of course abolished: and further, that the very Statute itself, empowering his Majesty to erect the Supreme Court of Judicature, forbids, on the severest penalties, the Servants of the Company from carrying on any inland trade. Having no privilege, therefore, to confer on those natives, who before were solicitous to become their Banyans *, the reason ceases for including them within the jurisdiction of the Supreme Court. *Cessante causâ cessat effectus*, is the inference we should naturally make,—did not the whole history of this Institution, in every point I have been able to consider it, manifestly prove that it was framed for a different state of affairs in Bengal, than what existed at the time of its actual establishment;—that it was created several years *after* the real necessity for it ceased to operate; and in

---

* This looks as if the judicial and political parts of that Statute of the 13th George III. commonly called the *Regulating Act*, were drawn by different hands; – which was probably the case.

this light may be called, not improperly, a *posthumous* offspring :—That instead of rooting out the remaining abuses, the active principles with which it was endued, took a different turn,—and so far from securing the peace and happiness of the natives, it has introduced universal confusion ;—has loosened every band of public and private life * ;—has embroiled the Company's affairs, and impaired, and almost

---

* The effects of this Institution in private life, appear very fully in the Report of the Select Committee of the House of Commons. We are there informed, by the testimony of several respectable Gentlemen who have resided in India, that " the natives would nine times in ten rather give " up their property, than dispute it in the Supreme Court ; " —that nothing but personal and private pique against " one another carries them there ;—that they are in general averse to the Supreme Court, which proceeds upon " the strict formalities of law, with a severity perfectly " incomprehensible to the natives," pag. 61. 77. Captain *Joseph Price* observes, in his evidence, " that the most " intelligent natives he ever conversed with, had not an " idea of making a distinction between law and equity." Poor *stupid* people ! a lawyer would say.

I shall not add the many impediments to the reception of our laws, too rooted to be eradicated by force or persuasion (which Sir Elijah Impey himself has stated in an early letter to Lord Rochford) ; impediments which, in my mind, preclude the *possibility* of this Court's being of any utility to the natives; while all its power of doing mischief is left to operate in full force in those very respects. He observes, " that men among the Hindoos of a high " cast, and Mussulmen of high rank, think it so great a
" disgrace

moſt ruined, its revenues,—and that, at length, the unwearied efforts of the Judges, to enlarge their powers, and extend their juriſdiction, have compelled the Governor and Council to reſtrain theſe progreſſive miſchiefs by a ſtrong hand, and with an armed force ſtop the execution of the laws, and the proceſs of the Court;—a meaſure for which they were reduced, in the laſt Seſſion of Parliament, to throw themſelves upon their King and Country for an Act of Indemnity, and which they could only defend on the ſtrong ground of a neceſſity, that was either ſuperior to law, or was ultimately reſolvable

"diſgrace to take an oath, that the utmoſt rigour of the
"laws is frequently inſufficient to compel them to it as
"witneſſes; and that they would pay any demand rather
"than anſwer an oath to a bill in equity. A woman
"Hindoo, or Moor, if not the outcaſt of the people, can
"by no treatment be provoked to apply to a Court of
"Juſtice—If ſhe muſt make her perſonal appearance,
"there is no proceſs ſhe would not ſtand out, rather than
"appear as a witneſs—An accuſation againſt her, if ſhe is
"brought forth to make anſwer, is equal to a capital ſen-
"tence. The indignity in either caſe is ſo great, and her
"feelings of it ſo ſtrong, that ſhe would not, after what
"ſhe would conſider ſuch a diſgrace, ſubmit to live."
Report of the Select Committee, General Appendix, No. 32. After this, the extending our laws to this people, appears not only abſurd in theory, but in practice the moſt cruel and inhuman of all experiments that a wiſe Legiſlature ever made!

into

into the higheſt of all laws, " *the ſafety of the* " *State* *."

Whoever is at leiſure to trace the effects of this Juriſdiction, in the large and valuable Report delivered to the Houſe of Commons by the Select Committee laſt year, and compares the benevolent intention of Parliament on one hand, in erecting the Supreme Court, with the bitter conſequences that have attended

---

* The Governor and Council do not heſitate to aſſert, in their Petition to Parliament, that " the attempt to ex-
" tend to the inhabitants of theſe provinces the Juriſdic-
" tion of the Supreme Court of Judicature, and the au-
" thority of the Engliſh law, and of the forms and fictions
" of that law, which are yet more intolerable, becauſe
" leſs capable of being underſtood, would be ſuch a con-
" ſtraint on the minds of the people of theſe provinces, by
" the difference of ſuch laws and forms from their laws,
" habits, manners, and religious principles, which under
" every ſucceſſive conſtitution of the former Governments
" have been reſpected and ſupported, as might inflame
" them, notwithſtanding the known mildneſs and pa-
" tience which conſtitute their general character, to an
" open rebellion; leſs indeed to be apprehended in a time
" of peace, but certain in the event of an invaſion; and
" that ſuch an evil occurring in addition to the others
" already deſcribed, would add to the national calamity
" the national reproach of having deſervedly incurred
" it!!"

it,

it, on the other, will, if I am not miſtaken, find himſelf perfectly cured of the modern Univerſal Paſſion for tampering with Acts of Parliament,—and will ſee ONE MELAN-CHOLY PROOF MORE, of the inability and incapacity of one country to make laws for the inhabitants of another!

A REVIEW

OF THE

PRINCIPLES and CONDUCT of the JUDGES of his MAJESTY's Supreme Court of Judicature in BENGAL, &c.

IN the Introductory Pages that precede, I have been led farther than I originally intended, by an anxiety to have the true nature and constitution of the Jurisdiction, whose effects are now under discussion, clearly and accurately understood,—which, I am sorry to say, notwithstanding all that was written, and all that was said last year upon the subject, remains, in the minds of most, still clouded in a great deal of obscurity.

I imagine any very sanguine hopes the Reader might have entertained, of great and important benefits to be derived from this Institution,

ſtitution, are by this time conſiderably abated. Let us now proceed to examine the conduct of our new Judges, in the management of the large diſcretionary powers with which they were intruſted. Let us freely commend their conduct, if it has been wiſe and temperate; and remark their errors with candour, if their adminiſtration ſhall appear to have been as injudicious as the original plan was hazardous and doubtful.

Many obſervations might be made on the temper, character, and abilities of theſe Gentlemen*; but this part of the ſubject is invi-

---

* They were men of fair characters in private life; and the world knew little concerning them till the late complaints from India. If their manners have changed with their fortunes, or their ſentiments with their ſituation, the fact is not new in the hiſtory of human nature. The ſame man, who would make an exceeding good Recorder of a borough, may turn out a very indifferent Chief Juſtice; and, by an inconſiſtency of character not unfrequent, he who was moderate, mild, and temperate in England, may be violent, overbearing, and tyrannical in Bengal.

If great power and high office alter the characters of men, on the other hand they influence our judgment concerning them: And Pope ſatirically obſerves,

    " 'Tis from high life high characters are drawn;
    " A ſaint in crape, is twice a ſaint in lawn:
    " A JUDGE is juſt, a CHANCELLOR juſter ſtill.——

dious, and therefore, on all accounts, better omitted. I shall not intimate that such men were unfit to be trusted with any power; I had rather say, with the British inhabitants*, that such powers were unfit to be trusted with any men.

It is generally reported in Westminster-hall, that, on the first establishment of the Supreme Court, only five candidates presented themselves to fill the four seats, notwithstanding the novelty of the Institution, and the comparative magnitude of the Salaries †. When there was so little room for selection, it would be too captious to blame the choice; but we may surely lament, that so delicate a trust, and so nice and difficult a task as the application of our laws to the occasions of a distant country; a task which, requiring a masterly acquaintance with the general rules of jurisprudence (or, in other words, with those principles which run through, and are the basis of all laws), would have given fit exercise to all the abilities of a THURLOW, a MANSFIELD, or a LOUGHBOROUGH, was confided to four Gentlemen, whose only qualification (as required by the

* Vide Petition of the British inhabitants of Bengal, to the Commons of Great Britain in Parliament assembled.

† The Chief Justice 8000 l. per ann. and each of the Puisne Judges 6000 l. Stat. 13 Geo. III. c. 63.

Act

Act of Parliament) was confined to the single point of being " Barristers at Law of five years " standing ! *"

That such a trust required great liberality of mind, and very enlarged views (qualities for which our practical Lawyers are not in general celebrated), will, I think, be admitted by every man who is at all acquainted with history, and who reflects, that one of the strongest features in the manners, character, and government of Eastern nations, is the prompt and simple mode of judicature that has ever prevailed amongst them. I shall not pretend to resolve this into its causes; the *fact* is certainly so. In all the European nations, on the other hand, that possess a free Government, the administration of justice is cumbersome, tedious, and perplexed; with more of the substance of justice, and certainly with more of its forms.—Those forms are said to be the price a nation pays for its freedom; and have been considered as so many checks, provided by the jealousy of the people, to limit the arbitrary discretion of their Judges. In England particularly, the multiplicity of our forms, and " the law's delay," has been complained of ever since the invention of printing. It has been the favourite theme of ridicule, declama-

* 13 George III. c. 63. § 13.

tion, or of satire, as the writer has been disposed to be witty, moral, or severe.——Yet our lawyers and our laws have gone on in their old course;—the lawyers have generally swallowed the *oyster*, and left their clients only the *shell* *.

'With these opposite principles in the two Systems of Judicature, in India and in England, the former summary, simple, and unexpensive, yet with the risque of injustice; the latter more perfect in itself, yet attended with the certainty of delay; the experiment was now to be made, of *transmuting* these opposite defects, and of ingrafting our English forms † on the *Gentoo* stock.—Whatever was the real

---

* Vide Boileau, "Un jour, dit un Auteur," &c.

† The Judges have adhered to the forms of our laws, in trials between native and native, with a strictness almost ridiculous. The forms of EJECTMENT, for instance, one of our most technical and fictitious actions, are transplanted to India, with all the terms of *casual ejector, lessor of the plaintiff, double demise, lease, entry,* and *ouster*, &c. Even JOHN DOE has found himself upon the banks of the Ganges;—and I have read the proceedings of the Supreme Court in an action, with the following title: *Doe, on the demise of Narain Tagoor, against Berjomohon Sircar.—* What real transport would it have given an old English lawyer, of the 16th century, could he have foreseen the illustrious rank to which his old acquaintance JOHN DOE has arisen, in those distant Empires beyond the Cape of Good Hope!

intention

intention of the Legiflature, fuch has been the effect.

I fhall beg leave to recur for a moment to the Act of 1773, commonly called the Regulating Act, by which the Judges were appointed.—There were two parts of that Act, each having the fame general object; the Reformation and Prevention of Abufes in the Affairs of India. By one, a Governor and Council were appointed, in whom was vefted " the whole civil and military Government " of Bengal, Bahar, and Oriffa;" by the other, a Court of Juftice was eftablifhed, with the powers, and for the purpofes already defcribed.

Thefe two great branches of the Government, the executive and the judicial, the two mafter wheels in this mighty machine, were made perfectly independent of each other: they were co-ordinate in point of authority; each was fupreme in its own department; and from their union refulted a third Power, fuperior to both; namely, a *legiflative* power; for we find that all new regulations of the Governor and Council, regiftered in the Supreme Court, were to become binding in thofe provinces*,

* Vide Section 36.

and

and clothed with all the attributes and qualities that diftinguifh law as a rule of conduct from the caprice of defpotifm.

As provifion was made for the co-operation of thefe powers, fo the poffible cafe of their difunion was not unforefeen or unprovided for. If Sir Elijah Impey was confulted in framing the Letters-patent (as by his own confeffion* it appears he was); it is eafy to forefee which way fuch provifions were likely to operate. The Mayor's Court at Calcutta, which the Supreme Court fupplanted, was a Court of Equity. It confifted of a Mayor and ten Aldermen, felected from the Britifh inhabitants, who, not being lawyers by profeffion, governed themfelves by an attention to the merits of the cafe only; on which account it was a favourite Court with the Britifh inhabitants; and as they have had a great deal more law, and (as they think) a great deal lefs equity †, fince it was

* Vide Introduction. The Reader will obferve, that the Act of Parliament gives the King power to erect a Court of Juftice by his Royal Letters-patent, and only draws a general *outline* for the Crown Lawyers to fill up.

† One of the Gentlemen lately returned from India, who was examined before the Select Committee laft year, faid drily enough, " That before the inftitution of the " Supreme Court, they had very little *law*, but a great deal " of *juftice*."—Report of the Select Committee, p. 73.

F abolifhed,

abolished, it has been a still greater favourite with them:—but it was alleged to be insufficient for its purposes, from the narrowness of its powers, and from the probable partiality of British subjects in decisions between their countrymen and the natives, and principally on account of its members being removeable at pleasure by the Governor, and therefore exposed to his influence.—In the constitution of the Supreme Court, care was taken to avoid this error. The Gentlemen of the Council were made amenable to its process, though their persons were not liable to arrest, unless for treason and felony.—No exemption was even allowed for acts done in their public capacity.— And further, a clause was tacked to the King's Letters-patent, enjoining all persons, both civil and *military*, to aid the process of the Court; so that in case of a variance with the Judges respecting the extent of their powers, the Governor and Council, who were the governing Power of the country; who held the sword of state, and commanded the Company's armies; who were placed at the head of all the other British subjects in those provinces, were suddenly to find themselves naked, and deserted of all assistance: while the Judges were to be protected in their persons, their judgments to be unquestioned in that country, and let them transgress their powers ever so widely, or abuse them ever so flagrantly,

flagrantly, were to be subject to no controul, but by a long, expensive, and hopeless reference to Great Britain, from whence redress might come too late, if it ever came at all.

On the other hand, the Governor and Council possessed no small share of effective power to counterpoise these legal powers in the Court. They derived a living, active energy from their station, far superior to what flows from Records or Letters-patent.—The troops were more likely to obey the mandate of the Governor and Council, than a writ from the Judges, though the choice, which of the two they should obey, seems entirely left with the troops themselves: A dreadful option, when considered in theory, and such as I believe no wise nation set an example of before!

We see, therefore, the case of a rupture between these two powers of State was not unforeseen; though I hardly know how to say it was *provided* against.—Natural history teaches us, that animals of prey shew in their structure the purposes of their destination: from the fangs of some, and the talons of others, we know that they are made for contest and for bloodshed.—We may transfer this observation to the constitution of these two Great Powers in the government of India.

They

They were much better provided for contention than for union. We see the *dragon's teeth* were sown in their very structure.—Nor was it long before they shot up into *a crop of armed men*;—for within less than five years we find the Governor and Council actually employing a body of troops to restrain the violent proceedings of the Court in the extension of its jurisdiction.

The Members of the New Council, appointed by the Act of 1773, in order to give greater solemnity and weight to their Commission, than a mere appointment of the Court of Directors might be supposed to confer, were expressly named by Parliament in the body of the Act. Mr. HASTINGS, the former Governor, was continued in his high office, with additional powers; and Mr. BARWELL, likewise an old Servant of the Company, together with Sir JOHN CLAVERING, Mr. FRANCIS, and Colonel MONSON, were appointed Counsellors.—In all their public, deliberative acts, they were to be bound by the majority;—and in case of an equality of numbers, the Governor had the casting voice.

Unfortunately for the Company and for the Country, dissensions broke out very early in the Council. The three last mentioned Gentlemen,

tlemen, who went from England at the same time with the new Judges (and who may be supposed to have had the print and impression of the sentiments of the Legislature and the nation, on India affairs, still fresh upon their minds), acted together in a majority. Mr. HASTINGS and Mr. BARWELL, the old Servants of the Company, formed the minority.

Into the nature and causes of these dissensions, I have neither leisure nor ability to examine. It has been said, that the majority were over-zealous in the work of reformation, and by their violence and precipitation tended to unsettle the fabric of government, and throw every thing into confusion; and that on this ground they were resisted by the minority, whose longer experience gave them great advantages. In these unhappy divisions, the Judges (to the surprize of many, who reflected on the ends of their mission) supported the latter, and fell into their scale as a sort of counterpoise to the power of the majority. They were accordingly considered very early as POLITICAL Judges; a character which the constitution of this country disapproves, though the situation of India at that time might invite them to assume. A great proportion of the Company's Servants sided with the Court of Justice; and the

the popularity of the Judges was so great, that we find Addresses * were presented them from the British inhabitants, in expression of the blessings of this new institution. These Addresses the Chief Justice took care to transmit to his Majesty's Secretary of State and to the

* This was in the year 1775. The British inhabitants were then in high favour with the Chief Justice; though afterwards, when (dissatisfied with the arbitrary conduct of the Judges) they claimed a right of trial by jury, he held a different language; it then suits his purpose to load them with every foul imputation that calumny can suggest.—Vide his Letter to the Secretary of State in 1779.—Select Comm. Rep. Gen. App.

It is certainly true, that a bad man has the best and clearest right to abuse those who have formerly supported him. If he admits their support was ill-grounded, and that their motives were wrong in one instance, he may with some colour impute it in another.—The Public will say they were justly served.

It ought to be mentioned, that there were Addresses to the Judges likewise from the NATIVES resident at Calcutta. Of the real value of these, we may form some judgment from the evidence that has appeared before the House of Commons. One of the witnesses being asked, "whether he believed these Addresses were the spontaneous effects of their own ideas, or the effects of influence or fear? Said, he believed they were principally the effects of influence and fear, if not altogether so; inasmuch as he has been given to understand, from various descriptions of natives, that those who did not sign such Addresses would not be considered as the friends of the Supreme Court or the Government." Report of the Select Committee, p. 60.

Court

Court of Directors, as a clear and decided proof of the sense the Public entertained of the beneficial effects of the Court's institution;— though many considered them at Calcutta as nothing more than a political manœuvre, set on foot by the minority to gratify the Chief Justice and his brethren on the Bench.

From the moment the Judges appeared in the light of POLITICAL characters, moderate men, both in India and in Europe, scrupled not to pronounce, that the principal ends of their appointment were defeated. From the same moment, the little hope of this institution's proving of any utility to the natives, was entirely done away.

  " Ex illo fluere ac retro sublapsa referri
  " Spes Danaûm."

The trial, conviction, and execution of NUNDECOMAR, for an offence not capital by the laws of his own country,—though made capital by an English Statute; and the circumstance of it's being enforced at the critical period when he was exhibiting a public charge against Mr. HASTINGS, contributed to strengthen this impression. The natural misapprehension of the natives, that he was hanged, not for the forgery, but for daring to prefer a complaint against an English Governor, is

said

said * to have intimidated the natives from making any more complaints against Europeans

* I have been cautious in expressing myself; for undoubtedly a good deal of party-spirit has mingled in the opinions of men on this subject. With a very large description of persons in India, the execution of Nundecomar was highly grateful. There was no doubt of his having committed the forgery;—and the odium of his character, his great power to do mischief, his intriguing, flagitious disposition, made him a dangerous member of society. But, in general, these political reasons have not been thought sufficient in England to warrant the Judges in proceeding to enforce a sentence of death upon him; and they have accordingly been blamed, 1st, For trying him for an offence, not capital by the laws of his own country, upon the Statute of George II. which makes it capital, when they might have tried him for the offence as it stood at common-law; in which case the punishment is not capital. 2dly, For not respiting him (as they are expresly empowered to do) till his Majesty's pleasure should have been known. 3dly, For construing the Act itself (2 George II.) to extend to Bengal, when it is demonstrable that it related to the state of credit in England only; by its mention of Exchequer tallies, and other particulars, and by there being an express clause in it, that it shall not extend to Scotland—*a fortiori*, it ought not to have been extended to Bengal, a country which was not in the possession of the English till near 40 years after the Act passed.—On these accounts the Judges have been censured for this transaction severely, and I think justly; though I cannot go so far as some have done, in insinuating that they prostituted their judicial powers in favour of Mr. Hastings, in order to commit a *legal* murder, and stained their ermine in the blood of his opponent and accuser

ans high in office; and the same effect was nearly produced at that time which Sir Elijah Impey malignantly imputes to the influence and intrigues of Mr. Hastings in 1780*, when these two Chiefs of the Court and Council were as strongly opposed to each other, as they were firmly united in 1775.

I have been credibly informed, that the late Lord Clive considered the institution of this Court as a wild project, and foretold that the Judges would find, soon after their arrival, that they were sent on an idle errand; and would pocket their salaries very contentedly, *and do nothing*.

Another Gentleman, likewise a Governor of Bengal, being shewn the LETTERS-PATENT † (which were the instructions of the Judges), pointed out very strongly in what respect the powers conferred upon them would not only

---

cuser Nundecomar. Vide Letter of the Majority of Council to the Court of Directors in 1775. Vide also Letter of Sir Elijah Impey to Lord Rochford.—General Appendix to the Select Committee's Report.

* " It is not probable you will hear of any further exertion of the natives in support of their rights against the power either of Government or individuals." Letter to Lord Weymouth. Select Committee's Report, Coffijurah Appendix, No. 25.

† Commonly called the Charter of Justice.

be of no ufe, but be productive of much mifchief.—His obfervations appeared fo forcible to the framers of thofe Letters-patent, that a promife was made to curtail the powers fo given, before the Judges left England; but this promife was never performed; and the Judges faid, they would fend over their earlieft obfervations on the fubject, and then the Letters-patent might be afterwards altered.— The Governor of Bengal, to whom I allude, knew too much of mankind, to fuppofe the Judges would ever be acceffory to any diminution of their own authority: no inftructions of that fort were accordingly ever fent back from India. *Veftigia nulla retrorfum.*

That the Court has produced much mifchief, as this Gentleman forefaw, is, I believe, a tolerably clear propofition. That it has been of no ufe, as Lord Clive foretold, or at leaft of no ufe that can be faid in any degree to counterbalance its mifchiefs, is at leaft as evident. But it certainly has not been unactive in the fenfe the noble Lord ventured to prophecy; on the contrary, from the very firft arrival of the Judges, we find them engaged in perpetual contefts with the majority of the Council, and in conftant ftruggles for the extenfion of their jurifdiction; one fide as vehemently afferting, and the other as refolutely refifting, the claims

of

of the other. Mutual altercations fucceeded to mutual claims; till at length, inftead of Reverend Judges exercifing in peace the dignified functions of their offices, we are fhocked with all the violence of partifans, heated with oppofition.

In fact, a coincidence of events, which was wholly unforefeen in England, invited, and almoft *impelled* the Judges to affume a political importance, which nothing but the divifions of the Council could have nurfed to the fize it afterwards attained. We muft therefore place it to the account of human infirmity, if the Judges, having once tafted of power, grew intoxicated with the draught; and if, after finding themfelves nearly in the fituation of umpires, and holding the balance of power between the two parties, they fhould be willing, when this coincidence of events had paffed away, to maintain, by all ways and means, their power and confequence in the Settlement.

This power, and this authority, which they gained by accident, they have kept by conftruction; and it has been a conftant fource of complaint—1ft, That inftead of confining their jurifdiction over the natives, within the meaning of the Act of Parliament, they have allowed

allowed it an operation that included every native within the provinces of Bengal, Bahar, and Orissa; and 2dly, That under pretence of confining the Governor and Council within the line of their duty, they have asserted a right of inspecting and controuling their proceedings, and have designedly degraded the authority of the Governor and Council in the eyes of the natives, well knowing that every diminution of their authority is an accession to themselves of power and influence in the Settlement.

I allude here not so much to the declarations of the majority of the Council, which the Chief Justice ascribes to *minds distempered with faction* (though the respectable names of Sir John Clavering, Mr. Francis, and Colonel Monson, might well have exempted them from so harsh an imputation), as to the very solemn Memorial of the 19th of November 1777, addressed to his Majesty's Secretary of State by the Court of Directors *, who may be considered as a middle body between the two contending powers, and who, as the Trustees of the Public for the safety of those countries, had an undoubted right to call upon the Ministers of the Crown to apply a remedy to the grievances they stated.

* This Address was signed by TWENTY-THREE Directors out of the twenty-four.

If I rightly understood the Lord Chancellor, in the debates of Parliament upon this subject last year, the Judges *did* receive some admonition respecting their conduct; but he said, " that they were tenacious of their powers." In regard to the Memorial I have just mentioned, his Lordship remarked, " that in his " opinion a Secretary of State, or an Officer of " the Crown, had no authority whatever to issue " a mandate to controul a Court of Justice esta- " blished by an Act of Parliament;" and further, that " it would be even *criminal* so to do ;" a doctrine in which every constitutional lawyer will, I am sure, concur with his Lordship.

Yet perhaps this is rather a dextrous defence, than a satisfactory reason, for letting these disorders run their length; till the Governor and Council were at last compelled to employ a military force to correct the mischief. If the mandates of a Secretary of State were not to be risqued, was it not in the power of the Ministry, was it not their *duty* to have brought a Bill into Parliament for this purpose? instead of sitting *with folded arms* * to wait the event of these dangerous collisions between the powers of our Government in India; and, instead of

---

* Scilicet is superis labor est! ea cura *quietos* Sollicitat!   VIRG.

leaving

leaving them to themselves, to work order out of confusion, and a new fabric from the dissolution of the old.

It is hardly necessary to go over the ground I have trod before, to give the Reader an idea of the extent of jurisdiction assumed and exercised over the *natives* by the Supreme Court. Having stated in the Introduction what I conceived to be the intention of Parliament in making *any* of the natives amenable to the English laws, and likewise the want of precision in describing this intention *, I shall now content myself with exhibiting a summary sketch or *synopsis* of the real and acquired jurisdiction of the Supreme Court within the space of five years.—This I shall do in the form of a Table; for the better bringing the subject within one view. The Reader will possibly be amused to see by what ingenious contrivances (particularly by the aid of a certain useful engine the Lawyers call CONSTRUCTION) this jurisdiction has enlarged itself, and will admire the yielding texture of all words, that pretend

---

* When men are satisfied that the end is good, they are not very exact in describing the means;—hence the latitude left by the Statute; and hence the mischiefs complained of. The event has shewn the extreme danger of trusting a discretionary power to any Judge or Judges, on the presumption that they will not abuse it.

to

to set limits to a legal jurisdiction. It requires little sagacity to foretel, that, where a Court of Justice is Supreme in point of authority; where it has the construction of its own powers lodged in the breast of its own Judges, the smallest opening to any latitude of interpretation, will serve to extend its jurisdiction *ad infinitum*. Every decision becomes a precedent for those which are to follow; till, like the circles made by a pebble " stirring the peaceful " lake," they grow wider and wider, and at length take in every object that ambition can desire.

" The centre shook: a circle straight succeeds,
" Another still, and still another spreads, &c."

TABLE

TABLE

OF THE

REAL OBJECTS OF THIS COURT'S JURISDICTION, as marked out by the Statute of 13 *George* III.

I. BRITISH SUBJECTS.

II. NATIVES *directly or indirectly in the Service of, or employed by,* BRITISH SUBJECTS, OR THE INDIA COMPANY.

ACQUIRED OR *constructive* OBJECTS OF ITS JURISDICTION.

I. *Under the Words* BRITISH SUBJECTS.

ALL EUROPEANS, as well foreigners* as British-born Subjects, residing within the limits of the FACTORY at Calcutta, and its environs.

ALL NATIVES resident within the local limits just mentioned, upon the

---

* By living under the protection of British arms, Foreigners are certainly amenable to British laws.

same

same principle of its being a BRITISH FACTORY. Thus, by one dash of the pen, FOUR OR FIVE HUNDRED THOUSAND [*] natives, ignorant of our laws, customs, and language, are made amenable to our civil and criminal code, to our statutable felonies, and to the rules of our common law, in all their transactions with one another.

ALL NATIVES, not only [†] during their residence, but having ONCE RESIDED, at Calcutta, are liable for every thing done, or contract made, during such former re-

---

[*] Mr. Verelst states them at six or seven hundred thousand; but I take the above statement to be nearer the mark. Vide Report of Select Committee.

[†] Though this sort of jurisdiction may, and I believe is strictly conformable to law, its consequences have been found highly oppressive. A native of rank (the Rajah of Bissenpore) was seized at the distance of eighty miles from Calcutta, upon pretence that he was subject to the jurisdiction of the Court. Being dragged down to Calcutta, he was then (legally) arrested as a resident of the place, and cast into the common gaol.

(50)

fidence, though they may afterwards dwell in parts of the provinces not within thefe limits. This city being the feat of Government, becomes occafionally the refort of every man of rank and fubftance in the country.

II. *Under the terms,* INDIRECTLY IN THE EMPLOYMENT OF THE COMPANY.

ALL NATIVES farming the Company's revenues *, in the different provinces and fubordinate diftricts.

ALL NATIVES, being the Sureties of fuch perfons; who may be confidered as the *monied* men of the provinces. This conftruction † arofe from the power the Surety

---

* This adjudication happened in 1778.—It excited an univerfal alarm among the renters, or farmers of the revenues in the province of Bahar, who thereupon prefented a Memorial, defiring to be releafed from their engagements with the Company, if this circumftance made them liable to the jurifdiction of the Supreme Court.

† The native who was declared amenable, was Behader Beg, who appears to have been concerned as furety for the revenue of twenty-five villages in the Bahar province.

poffeffed

possessed of collecting the revenues, in default of the principal.

ALL ZEMINDARS connected with the Company's revenues. The authority and situation of *Zemindars* are fully explained in the Report of the Select Committee. They are a sort of hereditary Proprietors of districts, and possess a degree of power and influence, that the same rank or property can never confer in England. They pay a fixed rent, or rather a stated tribute, to the Company, for the revenues of their districts; and this concern with the revenues constitutes the doubtful circumstance of their being indirectly employed by the Company, which has occasioned many disputes. The Chief Justice has conceded the point so far, as to admit that a *Zemindar*, quoad *Zemindar*, is not subject to the jurisdiction; that is, if he collects the revenues of his diſtrict to his own uſe. But it is well known that they are almoſt all tributary to the Company, which depends on them for its reſources; and we find that one great Zemindary pays alone to the Company upwards of 220,000 *l*. ſterling *per ann*. Vide Select Commitee's Report, p. 45.

The direct queſtion has never come before the Court; but many Zemindars have been haraſſed with writs; ſome of them have been releaſed on paying down a large ſum for accommodation-money to the attornies, and others have reſiſted, by a military force, all attempts to arreſt them; ſo that a regular and formal adjudication has always been prevented *.

III. *Under*

---

* There is no doubt which way this queſtion would be determined. Vide Sir Elijah Impey's laſt letter to Lord Weymouth, where he contends for the propriety of ſubjugating the Zemindars to the juriſdiction of the Supreme Court,

III. *Under the Terms,* NATIVES IN THE SERVICE OF THE COMPANY.

THE CAUZEES AND MUFTEES, the Mahomedan Judges who affift in the Provincial Courts of Judicature, in difpenfing juftice to fuch of the natives as are clearly not within the jurifdiction of the Supreme Court *. Being ultimately paid their falaries by the Company, thefe perfons may be confidered as literally

Court, and of making them pay their debts, as well as other great men.

The Governor and Council, on the other hand, contend, that, befides the difgrace of fubjecting the Zemindars to arrefts, &c. " fome of whom are the defcendants of " men who commanded armies, and poffeffed the rights " of Sovereign dominion over the Ryats or vaffals of their " refpective Zemindaries; almoft all of them are indebted " in enormous fums, for old debts moftly accruing from " extorted donations, and from the ufurious and accumu-
" lated intereft of many years, but which are capable of " being eftablifhed in an Englifh Court of Law;" and that one of the leaft confequences of fuch a jurifdiction over them, would be a complete transfer of the whole property of thofe provinces (a concuffion too violent for an unfettled Government to bear), as well as a total emancipation of thofe Zemindars from the controul of the Governor and Council.

* See PATNA CAUSE. Report of the Select Committee.

in the employment of the Company; though it is difficult to conceive that a Mahomedan or Hindoo Magiſtrate was within the contemplation of Parliament as an Agent of Europeans. Vide Introduction.

By authoriſing writs to go againſt theſe native Magiſtrates, the Supreme Court, in effect, annuls their decrees. "No! " ſays the Chief Juſtice, " we claim no authority " over their deciſions; " we only proceed *in* " *perſonam*; that is, to " fine them in damages " where we think they " have proceeded irre- " gularly; their decrees " are ſtill in force." Happy, ingenious, ſatisfactory diſtinction * !

Such has been the rapid growth of this *conſtructive* juriſdiction of the Supreme Court, as diſtinguiſhed from what I call the *real* juriſdic-

* Vide Sir Elijah Impey's Speech. Patna Appendix. Select Committee's Report.

tion,

tion, which Parliament originally intended. I am far from saying that the Judges have always decided wrong in questions of jurisdiction; though the natural jealousy of power may incline us to suspect it.—Their decisions may have been in some cases the unavoidable effects of that latitude of interpretation left in the Act. But I think the Reader will see there was some foundation for the constant complaints of the majority of Council; and that those complaints are neither violent nor factious (as the Chief Justice insinuates), nor too strong for the occasion. "We will not (say the Gentlemen of
" the Council) take upon us to decide, whether
" the conduct of the Judges is supported or
" condemned by the strict letter of the Act of
" Parliament and his Majesty's Charter; but
" we are ready to declare our clear and delibe-
" rate opinion, that it is not conformable to
" the true spirit of the Law and Charter, or to
" the views and principles on which the Su-
" preme Court of Judicature was instituted by
" the Legislature: much less can we discover,
" in the proceedings of the Judges, any traces
" of that moderation and discretion which
" might have been expected from their wis-
" dom, and which ought to have been ob-
" served, particularly at the outset of a new
" Institution, and in the exercise and applica-
" tion

" tion of Judicial Powers, not only new in
" themselves, but derived from a Sovereignty
" unknown to the people over whom those
" powers were to be exerted. In a situation
" so full of difficulty and hazard, and in which
" an unguarded or precipitate assertion, even
" of the powers legally vested in the Supreme
" Court, might be attended with the most
" dangerous consequences to the State, we
" rather hoped for assistance from the Judges
" in the settlement of this Government, than
" had any apprehension that they would carry
" their jurisdiction to an extent which, as we
" from the first apprehended, and as we are
" now convinced, must throw the whole coun-
" try into confusion." Gen. App. No. 3.
Select Committee's Report.

When the Bill that passed last year, for explaining and limiting the jurisdiction of the Supreme Court, was agitated in the House of Commons; few, and very few of the Judges friends ventured to say that their conduct had been discreet, temperate, or wise. One Gentleman, who headed a very respectable majority of that House in the last Parliament, in declaring that " *the influence of the Crown had* " *increased, was increasing, and ought to be di-* " *minished,*" was unwilling to admit, and yet unable

unable to deny, that the Jurisdiction of the Supreme Court had increased, was increasing, and ought to be diminished*. It will possibly be said, in vindication of the Judges, that unless they extended their jurisdictions over the natives, the Court and its practisers would have little or no business.

---

* It was the opinion of many persons, who are the admirers and friends of the Gentleman above alluded to, that, in the debates concerning the Supreme Court, he fell below the line of his own great talents, and discovered too little of that love for the general rights of mankind, for which he is so conspicuous on other occasions; and too much of the spirit of a practising lawyer. Almost all † the Gentlemen who vindicated the Judges, were, or had been lawyers by profession; and, what was remarkable, they all set out in this business with avowing to the House, that their only motive for taking a part in the debate, was their private friendship for the Judges; a confession which at once destroyed the whole strength of their argument. This confirms a common-place opinion, that a lawyer being by long habit accustomed to speak for his fee, cannot speak well without a fee.—" *The breath of an unfeed lawyer*" was proverbial in Shakespeare's time;—and it likewise gives some countenance to Mr. Horace Walpole's severe sarcasm upon the great lawyers and CHANCELLORS of former days: Speaking of the respective historical writings of Sir Thomas Moore, Lord Bacon, and Lord Clarendon, " I hope," says Mr. Walpole, " NO MORE CHANCELLORS will write " our story, till they can divest themselves of that habit of " their profession—*apologizing for a bad cause* ——."

† Sir Fl-r. N-rt-n, Mr, D-nn-g, Sir R—d S-tt-n, &c.—Sir Fl—r only spoke a few words when the business first came on in the House, but does not appear to have taken an active part.

Except in the case of NUNDECOMAR, few natives exhibited complaints in the Supreme Court against British subjects * in power; and Sir Elijah Impey, soon after his arrival, took an opportunity of declaring, in a manner very honourable to himself, that the general reflections cast upon the Mayor's Court in England, were totally ill-founded; and, instead of finding all his time taken up, on his first arrival, in setting aside its decrees, that in all the causes he had any occasion to examine, the MAYOR's COURT had determined according to equity and substantial justice.—Such was the language of moderation; before he was irritated with opposition; or inflamed with the prospect of obtaining political consequence in the Settlement.

What then was to become of the lawyers of the Supreme Court, if these sources of litigation were stopped up? Or whence was subsistence and support to be derived to the glorious phalanx of advocates, attornies, and attornies' clerks, &c. who now began to resort in great numbers to the standard of the Chief Justice? Besides the many adventurers who

* It is said only TWO actions have ever come before the Court, for peculation and abuse of office; offences which, next to restraining the outrages of open violence, the Legislature had principally in view in erecting the Supreme Court.

were

were allured from England, in hopes of making large fortunes in this line, many persons took up the profession there, who had been unsuccesful in other pursuits. In short, they formed a very numerous corps, and it was natural for Sir Elijah Impey to consider himself as their patron and guardian. We find from his letters, when the business of the Court fell off in consequence of the disputes between the Governor and Council and the Judges, that the attornies of the Court presented an Address to the Judges, in which, after making very honourable mention " of the " attention they had been pleased to shew " to the promotion of their interest *," they humbly petition them not to admit any more attornies to practise in the Court, as business began to decline so rapidly. This Address Sir Elijah incloses, with a very pathetic representation, to the Secretary of State, to convince his Lordship of the fatal consequences that would follow, should the jurisdiction of the Court be restrained †. One would suppose, those Gentlemen had really a FREEHOLD IN-

---

* Vide Select Committee's Report. Cossijurah App. No. 27.

† Ibid. Cossijurah App. No. 26. " The advocates, " attornies, and officers of the Court, *who have not al-* " *ready succeeded*, will be reduced to a most deplorable " situation."—Letter to Lord Weymouth.

TEREST in the quarrels and difputes of mankind, or that they had a Patent Right to diftrefs and harrafs the natives! Indeed it has been gravely contended, that, as almoft all defcriptions of men, " both with and without capaci-" ties" (as Lord Clive expreffed it), had acquired great riches in India, it was hard that the lawyers fhould be the only clafs who were debarred this benefit.—The harveft was over! it was cruel to envy them the fcanty † *gleanings* of the field.

I believe it will be thought, the conftructions put upon their jurifdiction, by the Judges, were tolerably comprehenfive. Under fome interpretation or other, hardly a native of opulence and rank was exempt from it. As almoft all power in that country may be faid to be an emanation from the Company, who reprefent the antient Sovereignty, it was eafy to conftrue every native, poffeffed of any power, to be " *indirectly* employed by the Company."

' However, the great body of the natives in the refpective provinces *, whom their extreme poverty,

† ——" Where Statutes glean the refufe of the fword."
JOHNSON.

* " The major part of the inhabitants of Bengal fup-" port themfelves and families on fo fmall an income as
" 3 l.

poverty, more than the express intention of Parliament, exempted from the jurisdiction of the Supreme Court, were still left to their own laws, in the Country Courts of Justice. Under the antient Mahomedan Government, justice was administered by the † CAWZEES and MUFTEES, men learned in the laws of the KORAN; and when our English establishment superseded the old Government, and Councils of Revenue were appointed in every large province (consisting, as I have said before, of the Company's most experienced Servants), some little alteration was made in the Courts of Judicature. The presence of one ‡ of the Members of Council, attended by the *Cawzee* and *Muftees*, was required. The Member who presided, was called the *Superintendant* of the ADAULUT §.

" 3 l. 10 s. a year."—Evidence of Richard Barwell, Esq.—Select Committee's Report.

† The name of Cawzee, or *Cadi*, must be familiar to every person at all read in Eastern History.

‡ The Regulations for these Courts were framed by Mr. Hastings, as was mentioned before. They appear printed in the Proceedings of the House of Commons in 1772; and, not being annulled or altered when the Supreme Court was established, were supposed to have received the tacit assent of the Legislature.

§ Or Court of Justice.—*Courts of Adaulut*, *Provincial Courts* of Justice, and *Country Courts*, are different names for the same Courts, and are used promiscuously in most of the East India publications.

In

In matters of Mahomedan law, the report of the Mahomedan lawyers was to direct him: in queſtions of *Hindoo* law, the Pundits* were conſulted. If no objection was made to the report of theſe native men of the law, the preſiding Member of the Provincial Council ordered it to be carried into execution; and an appeal lay from him to the Provincial Council at large, and from thence to the Governor General and Council at Calcutta.

It was obvious that theſe Judicatures muſt be more congenial to the natives, than the Supreme Court itſelf. The points of compariſon between the two Syſtems are brought together in a ſmall compaſs, by a Gentleman long reſident in the provinces, who declared, that, " in " his opinion, the natives were much better " pleaſed to plead their own cauſes" (which is the cuſtom of that country) " in their own " Courts, near their own homes, at no expence, " by themſelves or their agents, in a manner " they comprehended; than to truſt their

---

* " The Hindoo Law Expounders, or *Pundits,* are a " very extraordinary ſet of men. They profeſs to hold " little or no property, and depend upon the community " they live in. Theſe people are beyond the reach of " bribery, and are reſorted to on all occaſions where " queſtions of property are complicated."—Evidence of Richard Barwell, Eſq.—Select Committee's Report, p. 20.

" Cauſes

" Caufes to perfons they did not know; to be carried through a Court, the rules of which they were totally ignorant of; in a foreign language; at a vaft diftance; and where, whether they gained or loft the fuit, they were fure of an heavy expence—He" (the witnefs) " did not mean to infer that they thought lightly of the Englifh law or its profeffors; but the whole was not adapted to their fociety, and was beyond their comprehenfion." Examination of Ewan Law, Efq;—Select Committee's Report, p. 17.

We find, very early in the Hiftory of the Supreme Court, traces of a jealous difpofition towards the Members of thefe Provincial Councils, both as Boards of Revenue, and as Courts of Juftice. The Judges, who derived their authority from the * King of Great Britain, could but ill brook the rank and confequence annexed to the ftations of young men, whom they confidered as little better than the clerks of a *trading company* †. As this jealoufy afterwards ended in a complete demolition of

---

* The operation *of the King's Letters-patent*; the founding phrafes of the *King's Laws*; his *Majefty's Authority*, &c. occur every where in their Proceedings.

† One of the Judges openly denied, that " the Company's fituation, as Dewan of Bengal, Bahar, and Orifla, differed in any refpect from the fituation of a common trading company."—Vide Memorial of the Court of Directors to the Secretary of State.

these Provincial Courts, and the erection of the Chief Justice's power on their ruins, I must beg the attention of the Reader to this part of the Subject.

Though the " governing, ordering, and " management of all the territorial acquisitions " and revenues" is vested by the Act of Parliament in the Governor and Council, one of the Judges declared, that " this was not *exclusive*, " but subject to the jurisdiction of the King's " Court, and that it would be equally penal " in the Company, or in those acting under " them, to disobey the orders, and mandatory " process of the Court, in matters which " merely concern the Revenues, as in any " other matter or thing whatsoever *."

Accordingly numberless writs of *Habeas Corpus*, and other mandatory process, were issued, at different times, to the Councils of Revenue; and many debtors of the Company, in custody for large sums, discharged by the Supreme Court. In one of the returns from the Provincial Chief and Council of Dacca to a *Habeas Corpus*, stating, *that the person was detained under the order of the Provincial Chief and Council of Revenue* at DACCA, Mr. Justice Le Maistre exclaimed, " Who are the Provincial Chief and Council

* Memorial of the Court of Directors, No. 3. Appendix to the Select Committee's Report.

" of

"of Dacca? They are no Corporation in the eye of the law.—The Chief and Provincial Council of Dacca is an *ideal* body. The return might as well talk of the *King of the Fairies*, becaufe the law knows no fuch body*." This is one inftance, among many, of the enlarged minds and liberal views of our Englifh Judges, in the application of Englifh laws to the neceffities and fituation of a new country.—The Chief and Council of Dacca are intrufted with the civil adminiftration of a rich, extenfive, and populous province,—yet becaufe they are technically " no *Corporation* in the eye of the law," their acts are to be held out as nugatory, and their perfons ridiculed in the face of the natives!

I fhall leave the Reader to afcribe this fort of conduct in the Judges, either to deplorable narrownefs and extreme profeffional bigotry, or to a fettled uniform fyftem to degrade the Company's Servants, and to obtain to themfelves an authority and influence, co-extenfive with the whole Government of the country.

After this fmall fample of the conduct of the Judges, in regard to the Provincial Councils of Revenue, the Reader will

---

* Select Committee's Report.—General Append. No. 9.

hardly expect more moderation when the Provincial Courts of Justice came into collision with the Supreme Court. One of these Courts was established in Calcutta, before the arrival of the Judges. This, however, was soon suspended: Like the Pagan Oracles, on the promulgation of Christianity, it was immediately silenced by the Supreme Court; which declared, that " no native Court whatever had a " concurrent jurisdiction within the limits of " Calcutta, and its environs *."—Yet, within a short time afterwards, we find the Chief Justice himself stating the ill consequences of this very abolition, produced by his own declaration. In his letter to the Earl of Rochford (then Secretary of State), we have the following passage: " From our want of knowledge " of the language of the country, and from " the mode † prescribed to us by our Charter, " for the proceeding in causes, they must take " up much more time than if they were deter- " mined by those who understand the lan-

* Select Committee's Report, pag. 71, 72.

† i. e. Taking WRITTEN depositions in every petty cause. This was the happy substitute for trial by jury.— As English Counsel alone plead in the Supreme Court, questions are put in English, and translated into Persian or Moors; the answer is then translated into English, and the native required to subscribe, in his own hand-writing, this English deposition.

" guage,

" guage, and might proceed, as the Country
" Courts always have done, summarily. Were
" the Judges to sit only on causes between the
" Black Inhabitants of Calcutta, they could
" not go through with one half of them. It
" would be of great ease to us, and of infinite
" advantage to the inhabitants, if a *Provincial*
" *Dewannee Adaulut* was erected, by his Ma-
" jesty's authority, for this town, for the de-
" termination of suits between the native in-
" habitants of it, where the causes of action
" shall not exceed 500 rupees;—if established
" by his Majesty's authority, they might be
" CONTROULED BY THE SUPREME COURT. I
" hardly DARE to propose the same for the
" chief towns IN THE PROVINCES AT LARGE,
" as the Legislature did not think fit, in the
" last Act of Parliament, to interfere with
" them." Gen. Append. No. 32.

Here, then, so early as 1775, we have a plain deliberate confession of the real motives which have actuated the Judges. They had no objection it seems to the Provincial Courts, provided THEY had the CONTROUL; and it was the struggle to obtain this controul indirectly, which neither Parliament nor the King had given them directly, that occasioned all these violent proceedings in the PATNA CAUSE, against the Mahomedan Lawyers of the Patna Court,

Court, which ended in the death of the *Cauzee*, and the imprisonment of the *Muftees*.

A memorable saying of Mr. Justice Le Maistre from the Bench, will throw further light here, who, we are told, could not forbear expressing his surprize, " that so many " persons should apply for redress to the " Country Courts, when they might depend " upon having *as good justice, or better*, in " the Supreme Court *."—This was spoken with the true spirit of a retailer of English law, who wonders any other shop should have better custom than his own.—But, unfortunately, it was not till after the death of this zealous Gentleman, that the triumph of the Supreme Court, over these Country Courts, was complete; when unsuccessful litigants in the latter were instigated to bring actions in the Supreme Court, against the English Members of the Council, and the *Cawzee* and *Muftees*, the native expounders of the law, who were assessors in those Courts. This was the substance of the celebrated PATNA CAUSE; the decision of which, by the Supreme Court, I never heard

---

*. These were his very words.—Evidence of Captain Cowe.—Select Committee's Report, p. 61.—Mr. Le Maistre appears to have had all the passion for extending the jurisdiction of the Court, and all the violence of the Chief Justice, without his eloquence or abilities.

any

any lawyer in this country mention with approbation, nor any man who was not a lawyer, without indignation and difguft!

The common fenfe of mankind revolts at the abfurdity and injuftice of an Englifh Court, which had by law no appellate jurifdiction over thofe native Courts, affuming an indirect appeal, by admitting perfonal actions againft the Magiftrates that prefided there; and firft difgracefully arrefting the native Judges; then exacting their proceedings under the Mahomedan law, to the ftrict ftandard of the law of England; and if they did not exactly fit this iron bed of *Procruftes* (as the Supreme Court was juftly called), punifhing them in damages to the amount of the property they decide upon: As fimilar actions were brought againft the Englifh Members of the Council, the whole Settlement took the alarm: they forefaw that no integrity, no uprightnefs of decifion could form a protection, where any part of their proceedings, which an Englifh attorney could call irregular, was to make them refponfible in their private fortunes for their public acts.

Yet it muft be owned, the reafonings of the Judges are ingenious and plaufible. "All "acts of authority, not warranted by law, are "illegal.—Satisfy us (fays the Chief Juftice) "that

" that you proceed legally, and we shall admit your defence." Under this colourable argument, the Supreme Court proceeds in this indirect mode of appeal. The fallacy lies in the word *legal*. The Supreme Court calls the proceedings of a Mahomedan Court legal, if they square with the maxims of English law; if not, they are illegal, and punishable in large damages. In the action against the *Cauzee* and *Muftees*, we find Mr. Justice Chambers gravely suggesting to the Chief Justice a case from BROOKE's ABRIDGMENT*, to shew that the Mahomedan lawyers had acted against a technical rule of English law, in pronouncing upon the merits of a cause which the Gentlemen of the Council had delegated to them. The Council at Patna, it was said, ought to have tried the cause themselves, and only have consulted the Cauzee and Muftees on points of law. Here they delegated both the law and facts (that is, the whole cause †), which they themselves were delegated by the Governor

---

* Brooke's Abridgment, published about the time of queen Elizabeth.

† It turned upon the forgery of a Persian deed. This, though a question of fact, turns so much upon a knowledge of the language, and the internal marks of authenticity or forgery, that the Council may be easily defended for referring it to the Mahomedan lawyers.

and

and Council to try. *Delegatus non poteſt delegare poteſtatem**.

Suppoſing, however, that the Council proceeded irregularly, yet why puniſh the Cauzee and Muftees for acting under an order of reference which had been criminal in them to have declined! What a precious dilemma were theſe Mahomedans reduced to! Had they refuſed to try the cauſe, they would have been fined by the Council at Patna. Do they accept the reference? They are puniſhed by the Supreme Court at Calcutta!

Incidit in Scyllam qui vult vitare Charybdin.

By one or two of theſe deciſions, the Supreme Court had well-nigh ſilenced all the rival Judicatures in the interior parts of the provinces. I conſider its juriſdiction, therefore, as in its zenith at this period, which was about the beginning

---

* The Chief Juſtice cited Rolle's Abridgment.—"Juſtices in Eyre could not make a Deputy by common Law, but now they may by Statute—So may ſome Stewards of Manors; but then, ſays the Chief Juſtice, that is by preſcription."—Did he expect the *Cawzee* and *Muftees* to ſhew a preſcriptive right, or an Engliſh Act of Parliament, to warrant their proceedings! In fact, the maxim, that "a judicial power cannot be delegated," and the technical jargon of *delegatus non poteſt delegare*, is not univerſal even in the law of England, as we ſee from the Chief Juſtice's own quotations.

ginning of the year 1779. The natives, who were before amenable to the Country Courts, might now be expected to resort to the Supreme Court in great numbers; but the distance from Calcutta, the immense expence, their ignorance of English laws, its repugnance to their own usages, and, above all, their terror at the power of a Court which imprisoned their native Judges, contributed to prevent the natural consequences of the Patna decision from operating.—To dam up the stream of justice in one channel, is the likeliest way to make it flow more rapidly in another; but as "the reverse of wrong" is not always "right," so the destruction of the Country Courts does not appear to have increased the business of the Supreme Court, in that degree that might have been expected.—The natives remained for some time in a state of anarchy and confusion; without law*, and without redress!

The Chief Justice perceived he had gone too far. The odium and unpopularity of the judgment in the Patna cause was too great; and accordingly we find, that, at the latter end of the same year, when an action was brought in the Supreme Court, by a native

---

* Vide Minute of the Governor General, 9th March 1780.

against the Provincial Council of Moorshedebad, who conceived himself injured by some of their public acts, he refused to inquire into the regularity or irregularity of their proceedings, and dismissed the native with costs *. This in some measure restored the legal competency of the Councils, but it did not restore the confidence of the people.—As the Gentlemen of the Patna Council had avowed their determination to appeal from the former decision to the King in Council, the Chief Justice began to be a little more cautious and temperate.

It will not be supposed, that the proceedings of the Court, in the Patna Cause, passed with the perfect acquiescence of the Governor and Council: on the contrary, they extended their protection to the *Cauzee* and *Muftees* in every possible way that the law allowed. They bailed them pending the suit; they were at the whole expence of defending the action; and though they did not think themselves authorised

* This case was so replete with irregularity, on the part of the Provincial Council, that the Law-officers of the Company were unwilling to defend it.—Vide Case of *Gora Chund Dutt* v. *Hosea* and others. Opinion of the Advocate-General. Select Committee's Report, No. 4. General Appendix.

to pay the heavy* damages affeffed by the Court, they granted a liberal allowance to the furviving fufferers in prifon, and fettled a penfion on the widow of the Cauzee † who died in his way to the Calcutta gaol.

From this time, we find nothing very interefting in the hiftory of the Supreme Court till October 1779, when the attempt to execute the procefs of the Court on one of the hereditary ZEMINDARS of Bengal excited a new commotion, and kindled a frefh flame, in which all the leffer fires were extinguifhed or loft.

I have before mentioned that the ZEMINDARS were a fpecies of tributary Lords, or great landholders, who were anfwerable to the

---

* The property which they decided upon, as Judges of the Patna Court, was made the meafure of damages affeffed againft them, as individuals, amounting to the fum of 30,000 l. fterling, no part of which property ever came to their hands. As thefe unfortunate men had no other income but their offices, the fentence was equivalent to perpetual imprifonment.—Such are the benefits the natives reap from trials without a jury!

† This man was much refpected and beloved at Patna. He was appointed to the office of Cauzee in 1767; a time when Sir Elijah Impey as little expected to be Chief Juftice of Bengal, as the Cauzee did to be Chief Juftice of England.

Company for the revenues or rents of their diſtricts; and that, except the ſingle circumſtance of remitting their revenues * to the Company, they had no ſort of connection with the Engliſh government, language, or laws.

No deciſion had yet poſitively declared them amenable to the Supreme Court; but I believe a common Ejectment had once been brought, to obtain poſſeſſion of an antient Zemindary, which was wiſely compromiſed by the Governor before any great alarm was excited. Actions of other kinds had likewiſe been brought; but it was generally for the purpoſe of ſqueezing a little money from the Zemindars, and then they were releaſed before the queſtion was tried.

This queſtion, however, was ſeriouſly intended to be litigated, in the caſe of the *Rajah of Coſſijurah* †. A writ, for the large ſum of

---

* I obſerved before, that one of theſe great Zemindaries pays to the Company upwards of 220,000 l. a year (that is nearly five times as much as the whole kingdom of Scotland pays towards the land-tax of Great Britain). It is 13,000 ſquare miles in extent, and is held by a Princeſs, in her own right, called the *Ranny* of Rajaſhahi.

† Vide a minute detail of this diſpute in the Select Committee's Report, and Coſſijurah Appendix.

3,000,000

3,000,000 of rupees *, was actually issued out to arrest him at his palace, timely notice of which was given † to the Governor and Council, and application made to protect the Zemindar, who had absconded to avoid the disgrace of an arrest. Being clearly of opinion that the Zemindar was not within the jurisdiction, the Governor and Council gave him notice to pay no regard to the writ.—The Court proceeded to enforce their process, by a writ of sequestration; upon which the natives, who are devotedly attached to their ZEMINDARS, rose in his defence, and insulted the Sheriff's Officers.—A re-inforcement was held necessary by the Sheriff; and 86 men, armed with bludgeons, cutlasses, muskets, &c. repaired by his order to Cossijurah, entered the Rajah's house or palace, broke open the women's apartments, which are ever held sacred in that country, profaned his temple, and thrust the image of his worship into a basket, and deposited it, with mixed lumber, under the seal of the Court ‡.

The

---

* 330,000 l. sterling.

† By the Company's Collector at Midnapore.

‡ " Such acts are accounted instances of the grossest vi-
" olation and sacrilege, according to the principles and
" persuasions of the inhabitants of those provinces, and
" have been never known to have been authorised, with
" impunity,

The Governor and Council now thought it incumbent upon them to interfere, and put a stop to those violences, by sending a military force to apprehend the Sheriff's people; and the whole 86 men were accordingly obliged to capitulate, and were conducted by the victorious troops to Calcutta, as prisoners of war.

What was the conduct of Sir Elijah Impey and his associates on this occasion?— Enraged at the resistance shewn to their writ, and the authority of the Court, we are told they immediately declared their resolution of inflicting exemplary punishment on all who were suspected of being concerned in it. " With " an undistinguishing vengeance *" (say the Governor and Council) " they ordered attach- " ments to issue against the military Officer, " whose duty it was to execute the orders of " his superiors; on Mr. Naylor, the Com-

" impunity, by the most despotic of their Mahomedan " Rulers."—Petition of the Governor and Council to Parliament.

* These are strong expressions.—A respectable Senator (a Lawyer) observed, that it was indecent language; a Court of Justice, he said, was incapable of being actuated with sentiments of vengeance. This is true as a *dictum* of law, but it is not true as a matter of fact. A Court of Justice cannot feel personal resentment; but I believe the Reader will be of opinion that its Judges can.
" pany's

" pany's Attorney; and on Mr. Swainston, a
" Servant of the Company, whose only offence
" seems to have been an unfortunate curiosity,
" which led him to be a spectator of what the
" Court termed a rescue *." It appears to
have been thought too bold an effort to attack
the Governor and Council at once; the Judges
were therefore content, for the present, to hurl
the thunders of the law upon the Instruments
or Agents they had employed. This was an-
swering the same end; and knowing that the
Council could no more act without agents,
than a man can run without his feet, or fight
without hands, they were resolved to deter
others, by the severity of their proceedings,
from assisting upon the like occasions.

As Mr. Naylor was an attorney of the Court,
he seems naturally to have fallen within the scope
of their vengeance; but the attempt to punish
an Officer of the army, for obeying a military
command, was indeed a wild and frantic attempt, especially considering the representations the Chief Justice himself makes of the
contumacious spirit of the Company's army in
Bengal, in that most malignant letter of his to
the Secretary of State, in March 1779, on the

---

* Petition to Parliament.

conduct

conduct and difpofition of the Britifh Sub-jects. Select Comm. Rep.

Mr. Naylor was thrown into prifon, and ordered to anfwer to Interrogatories for a contempt of the Court. This unfortunate man was at that time in an infirm ftate of health; and the agitation of his mind, the unhealthy fituation of the gaol, and the terrors of the Court concurring, proved fatal to his conftitution*; he died foon after his releafe.

The

---

* Mr. Naylor appears to have been a young man of abilities. He juftly obferves, upon this mode of proceeding upon interrogatories, that "if there exifts a cafe, in " which the proceedings of a Court of Juftice fhould be " peculiarly temperate and forbearing, it is in that of an " Attachment for a fuppofed contempt of its authority; as " by one of thofe defects, which are common to all infti-" tutions, in that procefs the meafure of punifhment re-" mains in thofe hands, from which a difpenfation of it, " wholly difpaffionate, can hardly be expected: it par-" takes, befides, too ftrongly of that exercife of inqui-" fitional powers, which has been long banifhed from our " Courts; and though the dread of innovation has ftill left " this mark of defpotifm upon our law, the Judges of later " times have exercifed it with lenity and caution." Select Committee's Report, Coffijurah Appendix, No. 21.

After thefe juft and fpirited fentiments, it is hardly neceffary to fubjoin the authority of Lord Coke, in his celebrated comment upon the following lines of Virgil:

" Gnoffius hæc Rhadamanthus habet duriffima regna
" Caftigatque, auditque dolos, fubigitque, fateri."

" Firft

—The Chief Juſtice intimated, that, in a recent caſe * of contempt in England, a man had been confined two years, for refuſing to anſwer to interrogatories.—Such a length of confinement, the Governor and Council obſerve, or even a durance of two months in that unwholeſome climate, and in the foul air of a Calcutta gaol, would be equal to a direct ſentence of death †.

The Chief Juſtice, indeed, " appears to " *have loſt all temper* ‡ on this occaſion." In excuſe for him, it may be ſaid, that this was the only way in which he could vindicate the authority of the Court and the laws. If this were the only way, he certainly wanted not ſpi-

---

" Firſt, ſays he, he puniſheth, and then he heareth, and laſtly " compelleth to confeſs ; and makes and marrs laws at his " pleaſure." Theſe, he obſerves in the quaint language of his time, are " the damnable and damned proceedings " of hell."—Lord Coke was a better Lawyer than a Critic. Vide the Commentators on this paſſage of Virgil.

* Alluding, it is ſuppoſed, to the caſe of Mr. Bingley, who ſaid *he would never anſwer unleſs he was put to the torture*. The Court of King's Bench at laſt let him go without anſwering.

† Select Committee's Report, Coſſijurah Appendix, No. 23.

‡ The expreſſion of Mr. Rous (ſtanding Council to the Company), in his Report to the Court of Directors. Select Committee's Report, General Appendix.

rit

rit to tread in it; for we find him, in the following declaration, throwing defiance at the Governor and Council. "Whatever may be "their reasons" (says he), "and however ad- "vised to carry them into execution, I take "this first opportunity to declare, that no ter- "ror of power shall in the least intimidate me, "from granting attachments against any persons "who shall disobey the process of the Court. It "is in the power of the Governor General "and Council to prevent their execution; "but I mean to fling the utmost responsibility "upon those who support these ideas. I will "not shrink from my purpose. I have no au- "thority to command troops; but I can put "those who do command them into a situa- "tion to answer to his Majesty for the con- "tempt of his Authority *." And in another stage of the same proceeding, he declares, he never will submit to have his power controuled by any authority in that country, and much less by the Governor and Council. "We are "no politicians" (says he); "I have seldom "known lawyers good ones." [Some of his friends, high in the law, in England, will no doubt thank him for this intimation]. "We "have but one line to direct our conduct by; "and that is the Charter." And he then

* Select Committee's Report.

briefly

briefly insists on the qualities of an upright and independent Judge, and concludes with the following spirited (though rather hacknied) quotation from Horace.

" Justum et tenacem propositi virum,
" Non civium ardor prava jubentium,
" Non vultus instantis tyranni *
 " Mente quatit solidâ.

As it does not appear that the Chief Justice favoured his hearers, whether English, Mahomedan, or Gentoo, with a translation of these well quoted lines from Horace, I shall supply this defect, in part, by presenting the *English* Reader with Mr. Addison's spirited version.

The man resolv'd, and steady to his trust,
Inflexible to ill, and obstinately just,
May the rude rabble's insolence despise,
Their senseless clamours and tumultuous cries!
The tyrant's fierceness he beguiles,
And the stern brow and the harsh voice defies,
And with superior greatness smiles †.

It

---

* Meaning the Governor General. Qu.?

† Comparing the passage, in which the Chief Justice says, " I will not shrink from my purpose; I have no au-
" thority to command troops; but I can put those who
" do command them into a situation, &c." with the preceding

It is impossible not to admire the spirit and magnanimity of this great Chief Justice, or to refrain from expressing one's regret that he did not live in those early times, when the question of SHIP-MONEY, and other great political questions were agitated in this country, and in which a portion of his independent spirit, upon the English Bench, would have been more useful (and more applauded too!) than it has probably been at Calcutta.

In this state of collision remained the two great co-ordinate powers of our Government in the East. Mr. Hastings at the head of the Council, and Sir Elijah Impey at the head of the Court, like the two Roman Chiefs, one disdaining any equal, and the other any superior.—Nor were the inhabitants, native and British, uninterested * spec-

---

ceding lines of Horace, perhaps the following may be thought a closer translation than even Mr. Addison's.

The J-DGE resolv'd, and steady to his cause,
Who wields the thunder of the British laws;
Unshaken hears the suffering Indian's cries,
Mocks th' embattled troops, and H-ST—GS' threats defies.

* See a lively account of the general disgust, excited by the conduct of the Judges, in a late pamphlet, intitled, " An Extract of an Original Letter from Calcutta."

tators

tators of the contest:—Their passions were warmly engaged; while the Chief Justice, on the one hand, with his Latin and his law, his attachments and his sequestrations; and the Governor and Council, on the other, with the sword half unsheathed, were marshalled in hostile array.

In March 1780, each side transmitted strong representations to England, of the rise and progress of these disputes: the Chief Justice to the Secretary of State; the Governor and Council to the Court of Directors*. The Governor and Council inclosed a petition to Parliament, praying a Bill of Indemnity, for resisting, by open force, the ordinary course of justice (no light offence in the eye of the law, and perhaps amounting in strictness to high treason); and Sir Elijah Impey, on the other hand, calling for reparation at the hands of his Majesty's Ministers, for the violence offered to the King's Laws, Authority, and Government; and at the same time transmitting the Memorial (already alluded to) from the attornies of the Supreme Court, representing the alarming decline of

---

* Like separate streams, each recurring to the *fountain* of its authority.

business

business in consequence of the proceedings of the Council.

It does not appear that either party had candour enough to communicate their charges to each other, previous to transmitting them to England. The dispatches of both, however, appear printed in the Select Committee's Report; and the Reader, if he chuses to compare them, will find himself not a little staggered by the boldness of assertion, and the imposing strength of argument on each side. I do not say he will be " at a loss" (as Hobbes said of the controversy between Salmasius and Milton) " to decide whose language * is best, and
" whose

---

* I believe, in point of elegance of language, if this were a matter of any importance, the scale turns in favour of the Governor and Council; though the latter (remembering whom they write to) do not deal quite so much in Latin as the Chief Justice.—The following passage, among many, in the Letters of the Governor and Council on this affair, appears to me to be written in a manly and vigorous style:—" We have to lament, that in few, if any instances, the Judges have appeared solicitous to adapt the practice to the place; or seem aware of the consideration, that, though under an ancient, well-established constitution, which has advanced to perfection through the wisdom and experience of ages, the laws will execute themselves, and the stream of public justice find its channel, yet in a situation such as they act in, cases must often occur, to which,

if

"whose arguments are worst;"—nor perhaps will it be quite fair to believe all the ill they say of each other, or to reject all the handsome things they say of themselves.

By what strange revolution it happened, that all these strifes and animosities were suddenly composed at Calcutta, and, whilst the subject was under the anxious deliberation of Parliament, an union was in the mean time effected, more extraordinary than the former rupture, now remains to be explained.

We have already seen the Country Courts of Judicature prostrate at the feet of the Supreme Court; we have seen the Officers of Government embarrassed in the collections of the Revenue; the ZEMINDARS attempted to be drawn

if they attempt to apply the strict provisions of a foreign law, no force or management can regulate its course.

"We are not ignorant upon what unequal terms we encounter, in this matter, the superior learning of the Judges. Guided, however, in common with them, by the light of reason,—and instructed, in some degree, by the very contests in which we have been occasionally engaged with the Court; with all humility," &c. &c.' Select Committee's Report, General Appendix.

within

within the pale of the British laws; the Attorney to the Company imprisoned for resisting this attempt; and threats of similar treatment denounced against all persons who might obey the orders of the Governor and Council in the like predicament.

Besides the proceedings against Mr. Naylor, we are informed, by the Governor and Council, that the person who sued out the original process against the Rajah of Cossijurah, was instigated (as they firmly believe by the Court itself) to bring an action against the Governor and Council, whose resistance had prevented his proceeding in a due course of law.

The Governor and Council, on being served with the summons by the names of Warren Hastings, Edward Wheler, &c. (that is to say, as individuals), and conceiving it to be for acts done in their public capacity, which, under the Act of Parliament, they apprehended were not cognizable by the Supreme Court, refused to appear thereto, or to defend the suit; and further declared, by a solemn Memorial, which they ordered to be delivered in full Court, that they would not be accessory, by any act or admission of their own, to that state of degradation to which the

Supreme

Supreme Court of Judicature endeavoured to reduce the Government *.

On

* This Memorial contains the following paragraph: " Suppofing" (fay the Governor and Council) " their " prefent claim to the exemption they contend for, fhould " appear to the Court not to be founded in ftrict legal " right, ftill the Governor General and Council think " themfelves entitled to expect, from the prudence and " moderation of the Judges, and from the intereft they " hold in the general welfare and fecurity of the Britifh " Empire in India, that they will not permit fuch a quef- " tion to be agitated here, but that they will agree to " fufpend all proceedings whatfoever that may have rela- " tion to it, and fuffer the general queftion to be referred " home, as the Governor General and Council are de- " firous it fhould be, to the determination of a higher Ju- " rifdiction, or until the fenfe of the Legiflature can be " taken upon it; and the Governor General and Council " declare themfelves ready to accede to any mode which " the Judges may think fit to propofe, whether for the " immediate accommodation of the prefent unfortunate " difference, or for a reference of it to Parliament, pro- " vided that, in the mean time, all proceedings in this " matter be fufpended in the Supreme Court." Select Committee's Report, Coffijurah Appendix; No. 24.

One would naturally think, in this cold climate (where our animal fpirits are not fublimated by fo near an approach to the fun), that this compromife might have been accepted by the Supreme Court, without any lofs of its dignity.—No fuch thing! for we find the Chief Juftice, in his letter to Lord Weymouth, takes notice of this Memorial in the following fingular terms:—" Yefterday the " junior Council for the Company (for Mr. Newman, the " fenior,

On this unexampled footing rested the internal affairs of Bengal, in the Spring of the year

" senior, having disapproved of the proceeding of the
" Governor General and Council at Cossijurah, had
" refused to act as their Advocate in any part of the
" business), offered to the Court a paper, containing cer-
" tain Resolutions of the Governor General and Council,
" and moved that it should be read."

" On its being read, the Court, considering it to be a
" *clear contempt* of his Majesty's Law and of his Court, or-
" dered it to be recorded ; but, as it was in the case of
" the Governor General and Council, did no other act in
" consequence of it!" Select Committee's Report, Cossijurah Appendix, No. 5.

What raises our surprize here, is, that this very same Chief Justice, in a variance of infinitely less consequence, that happened in the year 1775, uses the most moderate and healing expressions. Addressing himself by letter to the Court of Directors, he says, " I fear greater alarm
" may be taken in England, from the apprehension of the
" consequences of a variance between the Governor Ge-
" neral and Council and the Court of Justice, than from
" the original matter of complaint, which in fact hath
" nothing of importance in it. I am so well convinced of
" the detriment which a variance would be of to the in-
" terest of the nation and the Company, that I will un-
" dertake that the Judges shall now, and will upon all
" occasions, act with the greatest moderation, and make
" such necessary and reasonable concessions, at the same
" time enforcing the authority of the Court, to the Go-
" vernor General and Council, that the State shall nei-
" ther incur scandal nor prejudice." General Appendix, No. 5.

Such

year 1780. The safety of the country stood
" trembling on the edge of law," while the
sword of State and the sword of Justice were
every moment ready to clash.—In the mean
time it was uncertain whether any, and what
attention, would be paid to the subject in England.—Three long years of dissension and reciprocal accusation had passed, since the Court
of Directors solicited the interference of Government to settle these disputes. No Bill had
been brought in, no conciliatory measures proposed.

It appears that the Chief Justice, from the
whole tenor of his conduct on the Bench, as
well as of his letters to Europe, thought himself very secure of support at home; and, indeed, as the Court of Judicature had been sent
out with the assent of a great majority of both
Houses of Parliament, there seems to have
been some grounds for his confidence. In his
disputes with the British subjects, he suffered
this *confidence* (to give it the best name) so far

Such is the language of Sir Elijah Impey in the year
1775, when he was yet young in office, and new to the
Settlement. The variance of 1775 was between the Court
and the *majority* of the Council only. In 1780, when the
dissension is between the Court and an *unanimous* Council,
we find the preceding overture of the Governor and Council treated as a CLEAR CONTEMPT of the Court!

to

to rise above all decency and propriety, as to tell them publicly that " he should take care " to transmit his own accounts of the Court's " proceedings to England, and should make " applications where they would be *attended* " *to*;" and in a private letter he addressed to Mr. Hastings (for whom he always had a real friendship), soon after the affair at Cossijurah, we have the following expressions: " When I sat down to write my letters for " Europe, I found myself so embarrassed that " I resolved not to proceed till I had another " opportunity of conversing with you on the " subject of Cossijurah."—And in another part he says, " Indeed, my friend, the em- " barrassment you have laid me under is the " greatest I have ever felt, and believe me I " should feel none were you not my friend*." —The import is certain; he imagined the Ministry would infallibly support him, and he was only afraid of implicating Mr. Hastings in the vengeance he was calling down on the rest of his opponents. This is the most favourable point of view in which I have been able to see Sir Elijah Impey's character; and as private friendship is in every state of life a virtue we ought to respect, I shall not detract from its merit.

* General Appendix, No. 33.

It is a matter of doubt (not indeed of any great importance), whether the intercourse of private life was ever suspended between these two Gentlemen during the height of their public dissensions; though it is certain the whole proceedings in the Cossijurah dispute were conducted with a perfect unanimity at the Council-board; "*an unanimity*" (they observe) "*not very usual with them*;" and Mr. Francis asserts, that the Governor often expressed the highest disgust and dissatisfaction at the violent proceedings of the Supreme Court.

However, the personal friendship between the Chief Justice and the Governor was always known; for amidst the fulminations of Sir Elijah Impey's eloquence in Mr. Naylor's affair, the Chief Justice, speaking in open Court of some conversations he had with the Governor, says, " I told him, the extremities I should be
" driven to, if it became necessary, would be
" most painful to me.—Gentlemen may smile,
"—and think I was not in earnest :—but I told
" him true; and no one has undergone more
" pain than I have, now matters have been
" driven to extremity."

I confess I should have been one of the Gentlemen who were "*guilty* of smiling," had I been present in Court; little suspecting, however, that a compromise was so near at hand between these contending Chiefs as it really was:

was:—but it seems the old adage is still true, *Amantium iræ, amoris redintegratio.* The Chief Justice might, for aught I know, have had it in contemplation, AT THAT VERY MOMENT, to accept the office of Judge of the SUDDER ADAULUT, which was soon afterwards conferred upon him, by the Governor and Council, with a salary of 8000 l. a year.

I shall endeavour to explain the nature of this extraordinary appointment as concisely as possible, together with the real and ostensible causes of bestowing it upon the Chief Justice.

For this purpose it will be necessary to refer to, what has been already stated, of the Constitution of the Provincial Courts of Judicature. I took notice that an appeal lay from their decisions to the Governor and Council at Calcutta *; who, sitting in the exercise of this appellate Jurisdiction, were called the Court of *Sudder* Adaulut (or superior Court of Justice), and had a superintending Power to make rules and orders for the good government of all the inferior Courts. After the decision of the PATNA CAUSE, the Governor and Council, either struck with the loud censures the Chief Justice so liberally bestowed on the informality, and

---

* In the same manner as an appeal to the King in Council is reserved in the different Constitutions of our Plantation Governments.

want

want of regularity in the proceedings of these Provincial Courts, as well as with his strong insinuations of their corruption and abuse *, or, more probably, desirous to restore confidence to those who presided, and to the suitors who resorted thither for redress †, framed a *new* set of Regulations; in which the line between the Member of the Council who presided in the administration of justice, and the rest of the Council who formed the Board of Revenue, was endeavoured to be more clearly drawn than had before been done. This, like all other innovations, was attended with some difficulties. The different parts of the new system did not perfectly harmonize; and nearly the same disputes, on a smaller scale, broke out between them, as existed in the larger sys-

---

* In the action against the unfortunate *Cauzee* and *Muftees*, the Select Committee take notice, that " there " was no *proof* whatever of peculation or corruption :" but the charges were confined " to their having acted " without a sufficient legal authority; to irregularity in " their proceedings, to their having pronounced an erro- " neous judgment, &c." Select Committee's Report, page 8. If the Cauzee had sat in judgment upon the *Chief Justice* (instead of the latter sitting in judgment on the *Cauzee*), we may suppose it would not have been difficult to have found flaws in *his* proceedings.—Who drew *the Lion vanquished?*

† The native suing for his rights, and taking possession of his property, under a decree of those Courts, is afterwards sued in the Supreme Court, and deemed an accessary to the trespass, if he is unable to defend the regularity of the Court's proceedings.

tem at Calcutta, between the Supreme Court and the Governor and Council. If these disputes had come to any head, there was every reason to expect the Judges of the Supreme Court would have stepped in, to increase, rather than to prevent, the confusion.

The Court of SUDDER ADAULUT, or Court of Appeal, however just and necessary it might appear in theory, was in fact never called into life and energy since the arrival of the new Judges at Calcutta. The fear of a collision between the two Jurisdictions had hitherto occasioned its suspension or inaction. In 1775, a correspondence respecting this very Court passed between the Council and the Judges, in which the latter admit the right of the Governor and Council to receive appeals; and that their decrees were not liable to be examined in any case wherein the Provincial Courts had a *legal* jurisdiction.—The Council thinking this an equivocal answer (as the Supreme Court reserved to itself the right of declaring where it was legal and where it was illegal), never exercised the functions of this Court.

After having lain in a quiescent state for so long a time, it was now likely to be awakened into exertion, in consequence of the disputes occasioned by those subsidiary regulations, just mentioned, for ascertaining the limits between the Provincial Courts of Justice and Boards of Revenue. These disputes took their rise in one of the largest provinces (that of PATNA, the old source and scene of contention); and all the parties were actually summoned to Calcutta, to await the final settlement of the Governor and Council.

The subject was, no doubt, attended with difficulties. The same jealous rival, the Supreme Court, was at hand, and ready to receive, with open arms, the unsuccessful complainant, which ever side should prevail. Such pregnant germs of discord could not fail of gathering strength to blow, in an atmosphere heated by the breath of so many lawyers.

The Governor appears to have shrunk from the impending task, which, to use his own words, 'required so much attention to these Courts in 'the infancy of their establishment, that they 'might neither prevent the purposes, nor ex-'ceed the limits, of their jurisdiction, nor suffer 'incroachments upon it.

'To effect these points' (says he) 'would re-'quire such a laborious, and almost unremitted 'application, that, however urgent or im-'portant they may appear, I should dread to 'bring them before the consultation of the 'Board, unless I could propose some *expedient*
'for

'for that end, that should not add to the
'weight of business with which it is already
'overcharged.'

I believe the public will be of opinion, that the measure the Governor proposed was a very extraordinary Expedient, and, like one of those dangerous remedies which a Physician offers to his almost exhausted patient, under a tremendous alternative, " either to kill or cure !"— It was no less than for the Governor and Council to divest themselves of their old constitutional authority, as a Court of Appeal, and in their stead to place the Chief Justice himself, the great original and cause of all the mischiefs they complained of; the chief actor in the former contentions; and *art and part* in all those violent proceedings against the Provincial Courts of Judicature*.

---

* It seems to be a favourite political maxim of the present day, and has even found its way into a certain great House, " that the same persons who have brought a " country into difficulties and embarrassments, are the " fittest to extricate them again." On this maxim, the Chief Justice appears to have been the fittest person to select for this high office; as best able, in the character of Judge of the SUDDER ADAULUT, to retrieve the mischiefs produced by his conduct in the SUPREME COURT; to administer at once the poison and the antidote; and, like the fabulous spear of Achilles, to heal the wounds he himself had made.

In the state of things at Calcutta, already described:—A vast majority of the British inhabitants in those provinces, having actually made themselves parties against the Chief Justice and the other Judges, in a petition then pending before Parliament; the Governor and Council standing in a similar, or indeed in a much worse predicament, in consequence of their open resistance to the process of the Court; the Judges continuing firm to their former principles of action, and the Chief Justice, in particular, like another *Jupiter Tonans,* hurling his thunderbolts at the devoted heads of his opponents;—in this state of things it will require very few words to prove, that such an appointment was not likely to be very popular at Calcutta.——Mr. Hastings honestly confesses, " he was " aware, the choice he had made for so im- " portant an office, and one which must mi- " nutely and narrowly overlook every rank of " the Civil Service, would subject him to " much popular prejudice; as its real ten- " dency would be misunderstood by many, " misrepresented by more, and perhaps " dreaded by a few." I shall be glad to know by whom such powers, in such hands, would not be *dreaded!*—Almost all the Civil Servants, who presided in those Provincial Councils, were (as has been just stated) at that moment parties against the Chief Justice, in a Petition

to

to Parliament, and on that account, as well as for the part they had taken in other tranſactions, were obnoxious to his reſentment. I believe it will be hardly ſaid, that the miſerable *Cauzees* and *Muftees* were likely to rejoice at this appointment and controul over them. It requires indeed all Mr. Haſtings's abilities to reconcile us to this meaſure. Let us hear his reaſons for the appointment, and (as he appeals to the rectitude of his own intentions) they have a right to the moſt favourable conſtruction.—' The want of legal powers, except
' ſuch as are implied in very doubtful con-
' ſtructions of the Act of Parliament, and the
' hazards to which the Superiors of the De-
' wanny Courts are expoſed, in their own per-
' ſons, from the exerciſe of their functions,
' has been the principal cauſe of this remiſſneſs,
' and equally of the diſregard which has been
' in many inſtances ſhewn to their authority.
' They will be now enabled to act with confi-
' dence; nor will any man DARE to conteſt
' their right of acting, when their proceedings
' are held under the ſanction and immediate
' patronage of the firſt Member of the Supreme
' Court, and with his participation in the in-
' ſtances of ſuch as are brought in appeal be-
' fore him, and regulated by his inſtructions.
' They very much require an inſtructor; and
' no one will doubt the ſuperior qualifications
' of the Chief Juſtice for ſuch a duty.

' It

'It will be a means of *lessening the distance* between the Board and the Supreme Court, which has perhaps been more than the undefined powers assumed to each, the cause of the want of that ACCOMMODATING temper, which ought to have influenced their intercourse with each other. The contests in which we have been unfortunately engaged with the Court, bore at one time so alarming a tendency, that I believe every Member of the Board foreboded the most dangerous consequences to the peace and resources of this Government from them. They are at present composed; but we cannot be certain that the calm will last beyond the actual vacation, since the same grounds and materials of disunion subsist, and the revival of it at a time like this, added to our other troubles, might, if carried to extremities, prove fatal.

'The proposition which I have submitted to the Board may, nor have I doubt that it will, prove *an instrument of conciliation* with the Court; and it will preclude the necessity of its assuming a jurisdiction over persons, exempted by our construction of the Act of Parliament from it. It will facilitate and give vigour to the course of justice; it will lessen the cares of the Board, and added to their leisure for occupations more urgent, and better suited to the genius and principles of Government. Nor will it be any accession "to the power of the Court, where that portion of authority, which is proposed to be given, is given only to a single man of the Court, and may be revoked whenever the Board shall think proper to resume it."

After reading these Minutes of the Governor General, with all the attention I am master of, they seem to me to resolve themselves into a plain and direct confession, that he was already too much embarrassed, by the proceedings of the Supreme Court, to risque any further contentions; that he was fairly obliged to yield the victory, and to own to the Chief Justice in the face of natives and Europeans,

"Vicisti, et victum tendere palmas
"Videre Ausonii:——
"Ulteriùs ne tende odiis *."

In what other light can we possibly regard his observation, that no man " will DARE to " attack the proceedings of the Provincial " Courts, when held under the sanction and " *patronage* of the Chief Justice;"—that this

---

* When a Chief Justice, to approve his independent spirit to the natives of India, cites an Ode of HORACE, I hope it will not be thought below the ambition of a Pamphleteer to convince his Readers that *he also* can quote Latin.

If the Writer should hence incur the charge of pedantry (a charge he would willingly escape), he commits himself to the Public with the foregoing apology.

appointment will *lessen the distance* between the Board and the Supreme Court;—and that it will preclude the *necessity* of its ASSUMING a jurisdiction over persons exempted from it by Parliament. This last argument is indeed one of those self-evident propositions, which our newspaper critics have lately stiled *Truisms*. " It will preclude the necessity of the Court's " *assuming* a jurisdiction;" How? By *giving* in express words that jurisdiction over the Provincial Councils, which for the last six years the Court had been uniformly struggling to usurp, and the Council as uniformly struggling to with-hold from them.

Professing to confine myself to the conduct of his Majesty's Judges, I shall not concern myself with enquiring into the motives of the Governor and Council, any farther than as they appear on the face of their public proceedings. If there are those who think that, in the whole of this transaction, they discern the traces of a JOBB, manifestly founded on mutual convenience and personal accommodation, I apprehend this will hardly be urged as a vindication of the Chief Justice: If, on the other hand, the advocates for Mr. Hastings succeed in convincing the world, that it was a wise and salutary measure to conciliate the Chief Justice to the Service of the State by a lucrative post, rather than provoke him to its ruin by maintaining the contention; I think this will prove as indifferent a ground

ground of defence for the latter, whose violent and precipitate conduct had made so humiliating an expedient on the part of the Governor, an act of political necessity. No law or precept enjoins a Governor to continue in a state of resistance to the authority of the laws, because he has once resisted, or to expose * his fortune and his peace of mind to the incursions of an hostile court of judicature, and his friends to imprisonment, and possibly to death (as in the case of Mr. Naylor), on the precarious chance of receiving an annual bill of indemnity from the Parliament of Great Britain; when he had it in his own power to gain the Chief Justice to his side; or (taking it in the most odious sense) to make him an *accomplice* in the transaction.

If we may believe the suggestions of a late writer, the only weapons that are ever likely to prove successful with the Judges, are those which the Governor actually employed, namely, " lucrative contracts to do nothing, " or sinecure offices with large salaries, revoc-

---

* There is a clause in the Regulating Act which exempts the persons of the Governor and Council in all cases except *Treason* and felony. But though their persons are protected in civil cases, their *property* is liable: and, if resisting the process of a Court of Law by an armed force, be (as it may be presumed to be) constructive treason within the clause of " levying war against the King," (Stat. Edw. III.), the situation of the Governor and Council was alarming indeed!

" able

"able at the pleasure of the Governor and
"Council†;" 'on this footing it may be
'presumed (says he) the Council would have
'no reason to complain of any want of pli-
'ancy and complaisance in the Judges. Here
'the matter will probably end, if the Court
'be continued on the present plan: and it is
'better it should end so, than that the King's
'Court of Justice should be avowedly resisted,
'or the contest between the Court and the
'Council continued. If the Judges are per-
'mitted to disturb and distress the Govern-
'ment at their pleasure, there is no other re-
'medy. The company must pay them in one
'shape or other, first, a great salary for doing
'mischief; secondly, as much for not doing
'it; and then the question will be, for what
'purpose should so many lawyers be quartered
'on the Company?' He afterwards gives a
short account of the appointment of Elijah
Impey to his new office with a salary of 8000l.
a year, and adds, 'The personal policy of the
'measure is not to be disputed. If there be
'other objections to it, Mr. Hastings may
'plead necessity, to which they who continue
'him in the government, should not reduce
'him.'

As the common motives of Policy are not always to be exacted to the strict standard of Mora-

† Extract of an original Letter from Calcutta. Printed for Debrett, in Piccadilly, 1782.

lity,

lity, and as the same application of the public money, which a stern Patriot would be apt to brand with the name of *Corruption*, may be softened into the gentle name of *Management*, I know not how far this defence will be deemed valid.— It ought to be mentioned that Mr. Hastings did not employ the last " prevailing argu-" ment*" till he found the *argumentum baculinum*, or open resistance, ineffectual. Having in vain attempted what could be done by strong measures, which like the North-wind in the fable, only made the traveller clasp his Cloak the closer, he then tries the gentler methods that were still in his power. The event is answerable. The Chief Justice at last relents. He is no longer impassive to the charms of interest and ambition †.

I cannot help remarking, with what indecent precipitation the Chief Justice accepts this place. It does not appear that he had ever enquired the conditions on which it was to be held: and it is certain, he stipulated no restrictions whatever respecting the controul, and no fence against any despotic orders of the Governor and Council. On the contrary, by his letter of the 24th of October, he undertakes the office, *subject to its present regulations*,

* Antient scandal insinuates, that there were certain arguments which made even Demosthenes. *Philippize*.

† " But when the warmer beams of influence play,
" He melts, and throws his cumbrous cloak away."

P   and

and *such other as the board shall think proper to add to them**: We see he accepts it, *non obstante* the Law of England; *non obstante* the Charter of the Crown, and the Act of Parliament; which were so loudly echoed before in his opposition to the Council. He forgets his own repeated protestations; his own boasted quotation from † Horace; he forgets even the petition

* A dreadful definition of the duty of an English Judge! and when we consider his own constant remonstrances against the Governor and Council, and his repeated insinuations of their base attempts, secretly to undermine and openly to overturn the King's Court, what are we to think of Sir Elijah Impey's accepting a Judicial Office, in which the measure of his obedience was not only unknown, but unlimited? What *sudden* irradiation had dispelled his gloomy apprehensions of the conduct of the Governor and Council, that he should thus implicitly submit himself to their orders? Was it not a little extraordinary, that his conversion should happen at that lucky moment when a lucrative post was offered him? — In vain will he urge, that it was a *voluntary* offer on the part of the Governor and Council: that he accepted it with a view to forward the Public Good; and defend himself in the words of King William, by saying, *Non rapui, sed recepi.* The world will judge of his motives by his conduct; the foregoing facts will be combined, and the obvious inference drawn in this country, where the theory and practice of political *arrangements* are tolerably well understood.

† Connecting his conduct from the destruction of the old system of Judicature in the Country Courts, to his acceptance of this office and salary, perhaps it were easy to find a more suitable quotation than his " Justum et tenacem propositi virum,"

tion of his Attorneys; for whom he stipulates neither provision nor compensation for their loss of business, at the time he accepts an office which the Governor recommends on the sole ground of its putting a stop to all claims of disputed jurisdiction, the great source of profit to the practisers of the Court. Indeed, the Chief Justice uses these gentlemen in a very shabby manner; when it is to serve his own purpose, they are represented as *starving* for want of practice, and he draws a lamentable picture of their distresses, and attends to their wants with so fatherly an anxiety, that instead of the Scripture History of the " Ravens feed-" ing Elijah," we almost fancy we see " Elijah " feeding the Ravens;" and thus acquitting the ancient obligation *.

Many

---

in the very same ode of Horace: vid. Juno's Speech, beginning with

  ——' Ilion Ilion
  ' FATALIS incestusque JUDEX
  ' Vertit in pulverem.'
down to
  ' Aurum irrepertum, *spernere* fortiter
  ' *Quam cogere humanos in usus*, &c.

* It is rather singular, that Sir Elijah Impey should expect to excite the feelings of this country, by a pathetic representation of the probable distresses of the Attornies, if the Court's Jurisdiction should be coerced. People are in general too much disposed to take part *against* the Lawyers, and to regard their complaint of want of business as

Many Attornies, it seems, in consequence of these proceedings, have entered into the army.——When the Supreme Court was established, some of them left the army to take up the more lucrative profession of the law. " Cedant arma togæ" was then the motto. This learned corps are once more returned to the former profession of arms.

Rurſus et in veterem fato revoluta figuram eſt *.

To return to the serious question,—— the Chief Justice probably did not expect the matter would ever come to an issue in the House of Commons. He trusted confidently, that

a happy omen of general good: just as they would the like representation of the College of Physicians, and the worshipful Company of Apothecaries, as a strong symptom of general health.

* Vid. Major Scott's Evidence in the late report of the Select Committee this Session. " The appointment of Sir
" Elijah Impey, he conceived, would effectually prevent the
" interference of the Supreme Court in matters of revenue,
" which was the grand article of advantage to the Law-
" yers, and that they must either get into the army, or
" return to England; and some of them had actually got
" into the army before he left the country.—— Some
" of the Attornies came out originally Cadets, and quit-
" ted the army for the practice of the Court, and in the
" late want of officers had been received again into the
" army."—— Query? Which is the greatest object of ambition, the post of Advocate General, or of Lieutenant-General? The honours of the Gown, or the Sword?

his

his friends in power would stifle all the complaints against him, before they got the length of a parliamentary investigation; and that the same authority which sent the Judges to India, would support them there in all their Acts *.

I assert this from a very attentive perusal of all his letters to the Secretary of State, which, if considered as hints or instructions for the private ear of his Majesty's Ministers, are easily accounted for. They are full of artful misrepresentations calculated to inflame the prejudices of those to whom they are addressed; and of strong insinuations against the Governor and Council, and against all the opponents of the Judges. I do not say that these misrepresentations are wilful on the part of the Chief Justice. Living in a confined Society at Calcutta; little acquainted with the manners and institutions of the country; and surrounded by lawyers, who had a common cause in inflaming his resentments, he might receive his information through a false medium, as well as feel a natural propensity to believe every assertion that

* It was made a loud subject of reproach by one of the warmest advocates for the Judges, that the Ministry had basely sacrificed the reputation and fortune of those gentlemen, by not supporting them in the last session of Parliament!

favoured

favoured his own wishes.——It happened fortunately for the persons who were the objects of his misrepresentations, that those letters instead of *lying* in the Secretary of State's office, or at the table of the Privy-Council, and distilling their poison in a quarter where the means of counteracting them did not extend, have been brought into open day-light, and have received, on the face of the Select Committee's Report, as public a refutation, as the aspersions were cruel and malignant. As to the contradictions that abound in those letters, I have remarked some of them as I proceeded. By comparing different parts, *inter se,* many of the charges are destroyed: by comparing them, with the Chief Justice's own conduct, they are all greatly invalidated.

One of the heaviest Accusations brought by the Chief Justice, is the malversation of the members of the Provincial Councils and Courts of Judicature. Although I consider the Chief Justice as an interested witness in attacking those Courts, and as having made himself at once Witness, Party, and Judge, I shall not object to his testimony. He says,
" In some of these Courts, as we (the Judges)
" are credibly informed, and of which *we entertain no doubt*; the administration of Justice
" has been let to hire to Dewans and Banyans
" of

" of those gentlemen whose duty it was to pre-
" side in those Courts; and those to whom it
" was let out, were left to indemnify themselves
" by what they could extract from the Suitors."
Such is the charge, containing imputations of the blackest dye; and unsupported by a tittle of evidence, unless the Chief Justice's belief is to be accepted for proof. The Committee that sat last year, justly conceiving it to be matter of the most serious importance, made a strict scrutiny into this point. Many Gentlemen of character and fortune were examined, who, having no intentions of returning into India, were certainly as unprejudiced as the Chief Justice in the inflamed state of affairs in Bengal could be, and certainly better informed of the institutions and customs of that country. And the result appears to have been a clear decisive confutation of this dark attack of the Chief Justice, and the reverse to have been as completely demonstrated as a negative can be proved*!

To

---

* Vide the evidence of C. W. BOUGHTON ROUS, Esq. a member of the House of Commons; EWAN LAW, Esq. Son of the Bishop of Carlisle; MAJOR RENNEL; RICHARD BARWELL, Esq. likewise a member of the House.

As the last mentioned gentleman was known to have been the friend and partizan of the Chief Justice, and as the Chief Justice intimated in his letters, a wish that Mr. Barwell might be examined on his behalf, his evidence

To confirm the preceding opinion of the design with which these letters were evidently framed,

evidence will receive additional weight from this circumstance.

EVIDENCE of RICHARD BARWELL, Esq.—Being asked whether the Members of the Provincial Councils, presiding in the Courts of Adaulut, were suspected of venality, or any other corruption in their judgments? Said, That the institution of the Court of Adaulut was calculated to preclude any improper influence in the European Judges: the state of society in England, and the principles that direct mankind, he believes, have the same weight over the minds of men abroad; but he does not recollect any instances of corruption in the Judges of the Court of Adaulut.—Being asked, if he had ever heard any instance of a Member of a Provincial Council selling the emoluments arising from the Adaulut over which he presides in rotation? Said, That he did not know of any; nor does he know of any advantages of office to be disposed of.—Being asked, If, from his knowledge of the country, he could say, whether the natives have confidence in the Provincial Adauluts? Said, He was of opinion they had: he did not believe they wished to substitute the Supreme Court in the place of the Provincial Adaulut.—Being asked, Whether he thought they would wish that their appeals should lie from the Provincial Adaulut to the Governor General and Council, or to the Supreme Court? Said, He believed they would prefer it to be to the Governor General and Council. A simple institution, and a direct and instantaneous administration of justice, determines this preference; for it must be indifferent to the natives, what set of men administer justice. Select Committee's Report, page 20.

EVIDENCE of EWAN LAW, Esq. Being asked, Whether he had ever heard of any person, presiding in a Dewannee

framed, I shall content myself with another short extract from one of them, wherein he insinuates,

wannee Adaulut, having farmed out the profits of his station for a certain sum? He said; He never had, nor did he think such a thing possible; for where there is an immediate appeal to the Council, it would answer no end: That if such a proceeding were to be made the subject of a complaint to the Governor General and Council, a severe scrutiny would be made into it, and the offender, if found guilty, would be dismissed the Service with disgrace. Select Committee's Report, page 19.

EVIDENCE of CHARLES WILLIAM BOUGHTON ROUS, Esq. Who being examined to the same point, in the administration of justice at DACCA, of which province he was Chief, said, That he not only does not know of any such practice having existed, during the whole time he held the Chiefship of Dacca, but on his conscience believes, that such a supposition is totally false. Had there existed such a practice, he thinks it must necessarily have come to his knowledge, and most probably would have been stated in the petitions of appeal; of which many are recorded in the Dacca Consultations, without the suppression of any circumstance contained in them. Select Committee's Report, page 29.

MAJOR RENNEL being examined as to the general estimation in which the administration of justice in the Country Courts was held by the natives; and being asked, whether the Cauzee and Muftees, and Indian Professors of Law, are in evil repute in that country? He said, He does not recollect hearing any thing for or against their characters; that he has often been in their company, was told the nature of their office, and has seen them treated with respect.—Being asked, Whether that respect appeared to him to be the effect of fear or of opinion? He said, Of opinion.

Q

insinuates, that the Petitions which the natives had signed against the jurisdiction of the Court were dictated by Englishmen; and asserts them to have been openly procured by the Agents of Government*. " The only manner,
" he adds, in which the obtaining Petitions here
" differs from the mode practised by factions
" in England, is, there they are solicited and
" got by influence, here they are commanded."
I mention this rather as an instance of what I have asserted before (that these letters were not meant to encounter a parliamentary inquiry, but are only fitted for the meridian of St. James's, and meanly calculated to flatter the prejudices of certain Great Persons there), than with any intention of controverting it as a mat-

opinion.—That the people of Bengal treat all the learned and religious with veneration; a veneration not easily conceived by those who have not been in that country, which would hardly be paid to them if they were considered as generally corrupt.—Being asked, If the natives were dissatisfied with the course of justice, as administered according to their own laws and usages? He said, By no means; and by what he has learnt from them, the administration of justice, in their Country Courts, is just the same now as it was under the Mahomedan Government: That he believes they do not desire a better, nor does he suppose they ever did, because they are so exceedingly attached to their own manners and customs, that they have scarce an idea of a better mode. Select Committee's Report, p. 20.

* Select Committee's Report, Cossijurah Appendix, No. 26.

ter

ter of fact, which, if it were true, would only furnish another proof of the total inutility of the Supreme Court, by shewing how unequal it must be to the *protection* of the natives, when it cannot prevent the operation of that power, which openly *compels* the natives to complain of a Court, which the Chief Justice asserts is their only barrier against oppression.—But can it be conceived, that so artful a writer as Sir Elijah, would have gone out of his way to cast such a wanton aspersion upon the leaders of Opposition in this country, if he imagined his letters would have been brought before the Public ? " The only manner in which the " obtaining Petitions here, differs from the " mode practised by FACTIONS in England, " is, there they are solicited, and got by in- " fluence ; here, they are commanded."—Is this the assertion of a man who expected his conduct would be defended by Mr. Dunning, Sir Fletcher Norton, &c. &c. ?

As to the matter of fact, however, let us see how it holds. On this point, I shall refer to Mr. Barwell's testimony alone, for a reason already intimated. This Gentleman being asked, ' If, ' before he left Bengal, there were not Peti- ' tions from Zemindars, and others, to the ' Governor General and Council, against the

' jurisdiction

'jurisdiction of the Supreme Court? said, Yes.
'And being asked, whether he thought these
'Petitions were the natural effects of their
'own opinions and fears, or obtained from
'them by the dread of the authority and power
'of the Governor and Council, or any other
'Europeans or their Agents? said, He be-
'lieved them to have proceeded from the
'people themselves, without any European
'influence or interference whatsoever; and
'this farther reason operated upon his mind,
'that no European influence had been used,
'as the Petitions are calculated to exempt the
'natives from prosecutions in our Courts,
'while Englishmen, of all denominations, are
'open to the attacks of the natives.'—Select
Committee's Report, page 58.

But leaving the Chief Justice to struggle in
his own toils, and attributing his insinuations
to the natural workings of a mind eager to
vindicate itself, and hence betrayed into asser-
tions which he himself will be the first to re-
tract, when the heat and resentment that dictated those angry letters subsides;——let us
return to his appointment of Superintendant
in the last resort of all those Courts, which,
publicly on the Bench, and privately in his
European letters, he had laboured to undermine and destroy.

If

If this compromise were still *sub silentio*, I am apt to believe the Ministry would be as little disposed to disturb its repose, as I am convinced they were last year to have applied a remedy to the disorders that prevailed before: had it not been for the vigour and activity of a few distinguished characters in the House of Commons. They might naturally entertain an opinion (which a certain indolence that hangs above them would be too apt to cherish), that the Governor had made a *good bargain* with the Chief Justice, by which, in effect, so much contention is suppressed, and so much money saved to the East India Company*. But the subject, with all its attendant circumstances, is now before Parliament. A decision one way or another must be given: And an appointment which the Governor proposed, and

---

* Evidence of Major Scott, he said, " He conceived " this appointment would produce a considerable saving " to the East India Company, by a very considerable di- " minution of their law charges, and by preventing (in- " direct) appeals to the Supreme Court in matters of Re- " venue, which he understood were attended with a con- " siderable deduction of the revenues. He had heard it " asserted, that the expences of this Court, and the " loss of revenues, had amounted to about a million " sterling."———

Sir

Sir Eyre Coote confirmed, as merely temporary, muſt now be made perpetual, or elſe wholly reſcinded *.

As I think it high time to put a period to this Review of the Principles and Conduct of the Judges, I ſhall wind up my obſervations here; preſuming that ſome, or all of the following conclusions, will inevitably force themſelves upon the conviction of the reader.

* It does not appear that the other two Judges, by any public act, declared either their diſſent or aſſent to this appointment. It is imagined they are to ſucceed to the office when Sir Elijah drops from the tree like ripe fruit; or when, like Elijah of old, he leaves his mantle behind him, and retires to Europe full of riches and honours. The laſt Report of the Select Committee concludes with ſaying, that " as far as appears to them," theſe two Judges had no ſhare in the tranſaction. But undoubtedly, the proſpect of ſucceeding to a lucrative office is an intereſt in reverſion; and, like other reverſionary intereſts, ſuſceptible of a valuation: otherwiſe it is wholly unaccountable, that they ſhould not have proteſted againſt this appointment of their Chief; and equally unaccountable, that the reciprocal charges of the Court and Council (each accuſing the other of ſubverting its legal authority), ſhould from this time be ſuddenly buried in a profound ſilence, and be remembered no more! Beſides, the Governor and Council have not gained a ſingle ſtep, if theſe two gentlemen chuſe to hold out: They form a majority in the Supreme Court; and then, how can the appointment of Sir Elijah Impey operate as a *Conciliation* between the two departments?

I. That

I. That admitting the Judges to have acted with the most upright views, and with the best abilities, it does not appear, after six years fatal experience, probable, or even possible, that an English Court of Law, proceeding upon the rules and maxims upon which they have proceeded, can be productive of any beneficial effects in the provinces of Bengal, Bahar, and Orissa:—That our laws, though selected with the greatest liberality, will never coalesce with the manners and customs of India; nor can we entertain a reasonable hope that they will, in any process of time, melt down into one consistent uniform system; they are composed of hostile and discordant parts, which will always fly back " with jarring recoil," as often as they are attempted to be brought into contact with each other.

II. That setting aside any views of private ambition, that may be supposed to have actuated the Judges, still they have shewn a narrowness of mind, and a servile attachment to the technical rules of English Law, which has proved them totally unequal to this difficult task of assimilating the two systems, supposing it were practicable.—To censure those gentlemen for a want of liberality of sentiment, and to convert " what is their misfortune into a fault," (as the common cant runs) may perhaps argue

a want

a want of liberality in return; but in a public question it is neither unusual nor unfair; and when the happiness of ten millions of inhabitants is put in the balance with the ease and satisfaction of three English gentlemen (however respectable in their private characters), it is no mark of illiberality to contend, that if they have shewn themselves unequal to the task they undertook, they ought to be recalled. We may at least be allowed to apply the gentle censure, with which a celebrated historian dismisses a certain Exiled Family from the throne of their ancestors*: " That their skill in go-
" vernment was not equal to the delicacy of
" their situation."

III. If, on the other hand, they have acted on a systematic connected scheme, to acquire an authority and influence in that country, and for this purpose have uniformly embarrassed the Company's leading servants, enfeebled the operations of government, and at length driven them to a complete surrender of all the power and influence of the settlement, at the feet of the Supreme Court †; if such shall appear to have

---

* Hume's Hist. of England.

† See Observations on the Administration of Justice in Bengal, published about a year and a half ago. " We
" must not wonder," says the writer, " that they" (the Judges)

have been their motives, and such their conduct; I trust that whatever may be their own narrow ideas of distributive justice, they will be taught to recollect a favourite position of the great and venerable Judge, who presides in the Court of King's Bench, "that it is and "must be true from the fixed and immutable "rules of eternal justice, that a conduct found- "ed in wrong, never can become *legal*, for the "benefit of the wrong doer."

IV. With respect to this late appointment of Sir Elijah Impey, with a large salary, revocable at the pleasure of the Governor and Council, it is so repugnant to every principle on which the Court and the Council have hitherto acted, that this alone is a strong objection to it. I cannot comprize what occurs to me on this head so well, as by borrowing the words of one of the learned counsel whom the Court of Direc-

Judges) "have been corrupted by power, since the best "of men have been so; we ought rather to censure the "institution by which they were exposed to so great "temptation." And with a prophetic spirit he adds, "I will be bold to say, if their power should increase in "the progression in which it has advanced to its present "bulk, that in the course of five years more, they will "form a TRIUMVIRATE, which no force in India will "be able to withstand." Pages 34, 35.

tors confulted on the legality of this appointment. 'I am of opinion, fays one of thefe
' gentlemen *, that the appointment is ille-
' gal, as contrary to the intention of the act of
' 13 Geo. III. and fubverfive of the object of
' the legiflature, in the inftitution of a Su-
' preme Court: I cannot forbear to add, that
' the example of a Chief Juftice, one day, fum-
' moning the Governor General and Council
' before his tribunal for acts done as Council,
' and the next accepting of emoluments
' equal to his original appointment, to be held
' during the pleafure of the fame Council, is
' in itfelf pernicious; and fhould this appoint-
' ment be confirmed, oppofition, right or wrong,
' to Government on the Seat of Juftice will
' become a fure road to preferment; and we
' may fee future judges leading examples of
' that corruption, which they were intended to
' punifh and prevent.' Vid. Append. to the
Select Committee's Report this Seffion.

V. It is a jealous principle of the Englifh Government, and founded in the foundeft maxims of liberty, that its Judges ought to be independent of the Executive power. It is the fureft bond the people have

* Mr. George Rous, ftanding Counfel to the India Company.

for

for the upright adminiftration of juftice, and is one of thofe rules that will hold with equal force in India and in England. For this the Mayor's Court was abolifhed, becaufe its judges were removable at the pleafure of the Governor: for this was the Supreme Court erected, and large falaries annexed by Parliament, and its judges nominated by a diftinct power from the Court of Directors, who have the controul over the Governor and Council. The Chief Juftice himfelf appears to have infifted on this circumftance with fufficient force in his recent difputes with the Governor. "Have "the Governor and Council forgot, that one "efpecial reafon for inftituting this Court, was "to protect the natives againft the oppreffions of "Britifh fubjects invefted with, and exercifing, "power in this country?" And very early in a correfpondence with the Governor, he lays it down as a principle, that the conduct of a Chief Juftice, like Cæfar's wife, ought not only to be chafte, but fhould not even be fufpected. "It is not fufficient (fays he), that "courts of juftice act independently; it is ne- "ceffary for the good government of a coun- "try, that they fhould be believed and known "to be above all influence. A maxim in "which I am fure to have the concurrence of

" the board *." If it be poffible to conceive more forcible expreffions in fo plain a point, we have them in his letter to Lord Rochford in 1775. " We will affift government in all
" fair and lawful acts; but we hold it to be
" our duty to maintain our independence;
" and I know it to be inconfiftent with the
" wifdom and juftice of my Sovereign and his
" Minifters, by any cenfure on our conduct,
" for maintaining it with decency and firm-
" nefs, to teach *future* judges to be obedient
" to the dictates of the Governor General and
" Council." Will this high-fpirited Chief Juftice defcend to tell us (upon his own prin-ciple, that a Court of Juftice fhould not only be independent, but be believed and known to be above all influence) how he could reconcile it to his mind to accept the higheft poft in the Company's fervice, revocable at the *pleafure* of that very Governor and Council, a poft in which, while he holds it, he muft be confidered† as fubfervient to their dictates; and as certain of lofing it whenever he acts againft the will of the majority? Will the natives repair with confidence to the Supreme, Court, whofe firft magiftrate is under the apparent controul of the Governor and Council?

-* Select Com. Rep. Gen. Appendix.
† I mean in every public point of view.

Or,

Or, in what light will the inſtitution of this Court appear to them after this compromiſe?

VI. In whatever point of view the natives conſider the tranſaction (whether they imagine the Court is brought over to the Council, or the Council is gone over to the Court), it muſt be a problem which their underſtandings can never ſolve. The whole is a myſtery, and one inextricable maze, without any clue to diſcover " where all the regular confuſion ends." We have given them in the whole Hiſtory of the Council and the Court, their quarrels, and their reconcilements, a lively ſpecimen of our Engliſh Drama, from which they will be enabled to form no inadequate idea of the intrigues of a modern comedy*. After four long Acts of diſſenſion and reſiſtance, of unnatural diſtreſſes, and wonderful deliveries; they now ſee the two principal Performers come together in a maſque; the curtain drops, and the drama ends.

---

* It will be difficult to ſay, whether it would furniſh moſt materials for the comic or the tragic muſe. The Execution of Nundecomar; the Impriſonment of the Muftees; the Death of the Cawzee; the accelerated Illneſs of Mr. Naylor, are ingredients rather of a *ſombre* caſt.

VII. As

VII. As to the Directors of the East India Company, the History of this Court must to them be an entertainment equally pleasant. At their request, the whole complicated machine was set in motion: And, after all its movements are displayed, it returns to the point from which it at first set out. They complained that they had lost all controul over their servants*. They sought and obtained an independent Court of Justice; and now, instead of a MAYOR's COURT, at little or no expence, they have a SUPREME COURT at an immense expence; and after six years experiment, in which period they have seen sufficient proof of the futility of all their former hopes, they now behold its chief Magistrate accept a lucrative post under the Governor and Council, to be held *durante bene placito*; and all ostensible grounds of this institution at once done away; while the court and its charges hang a dead weight upon their finances, like some cumbersome machine, admirable indeed for the multiplicity of its springs, and the curious construction of its checks and balances, but

* Vide Debates in Parliament, before the institution of the Supreme Court.

totally

totally useless in itself, and repaired and upheld at an enormous cost to the Company.

VIII. If the King or the Parliament had chosen to appoint Sir Elijah Impey Chief Judge over all the Country Courts, it had been a different question; but, from their not having done so, I conclude it was not their intention. And it will hardly be contended that he had a right to vex and harass the Council into the grant of an office, which the Legislature never intended him to fill;—or if the Governor and Council had given him the appointment, on his first arrival in India, before the minds of men (and his own more than any) were inflamed with animosity and resentment, it had been a less obnoxious step. But can it be thought that he is a proper person for that office, after all that has passed in the Settlement, and all that has passed in Parliament?

What complicated powers does this Gentleman at present exercise! If he was *Ubiquity* itself, he cannot perform all his functions. Not to speak of his Criminal, Ecclesiastical, Admiralty Jurisdictions, confirmed by the Letters-patent, I shall confine myself to his triple capacity of Chief Judge of an English *Court of Law,* an English *Court of Equity,* and a Mahomedan *Court of Appeals.*—It sometimes happens,

pens, in a Company of Strollers (to refume a former allufion), where the mufter-roll is fcanty, that the fame Performer is obliged to play three or four different Characters. On the Calcutta ftage, the fame neceffity has enforced the fame expedient. Sir Elijah Impey is the great Actor there:—Let us follow him through his different parts.—At one time we fee him in the habit and robes of a CHIEF JUSTICE, dealing out LAW by the ftrict fcales of Littleton and Coke. Lo! the fcene changes on a fudden. He has thrown afide his robes of ermine; and we behold him in a plain filk gown, difpenfing EQUITY* to

the

---

* The abfurdity of thefe fame Judges' prefiding in diftinct Courts of equity and law, is fufficiently evident. Let us fuppofe a judgment is pronounced in the Court of law in favour of the plaintiff—the defendant files his bill in equity—he obtains an injunction, and the plaintiff lofes his verdict. This indirect mode of appeal, from the *fame* men in red robes to the *fame* men in black, is a precious abfurdity. The old woman of Macedon's appeal, from "King Philip drunk, to King Philip fober," was really founded in good fenfe; though even that was but a precarious remedy.

I apprehend the Legiflature (Stat. 13 Geo. III.), by conftituting the Supreme Court both a Court of law and equity, only meant that there fhould be no defect of juftice from the narrownefs of its powers, and that, in their judgments, equity fhould temper the ftrictnefs of law: but the Letters-patent expreflly eftablifh, "that the said Supreme "Court fhall alfo be a Court of Equity, in the fame man-

"ner

the wondering native. Again the scene is shifted; and we are presented with the *Superintendant* of the SUDDER ADAULUT, reversing, confirming, or altering the decrees of the Provincial Courts in questions of HINDOO or of MAHOMEDAN Jurisprudence. In vain the suitor flies from Court to Court; the same Judge appears in all; crosses him like his Evil Genius, meets him in every avenue, and haunts him at every turn.

IX. But it may be contended, that Sir Elijah Impey's judicial habits, and knowledge of law, qualify him, in a peculiar manner, for exercising an appellate jurisdiction over all the Provincial Courts.—Without willingly detracting from the merits of a profession, which, when pursued on liberal principles, is the first and most honourable profession in this country; I think we may reasonably doubt, whether the habits of an *English* lawyer would qualify him for a Judge of a *Mahomedan* Court of Appeal.

" ner as the High Court of Chancery in Great Britain." By thus dividing the Courts, without separating the Judges, a new and enormous train of expence was incurred to the suitor, without any possible benefit.

If any thing can add to the perverseness of this Institution, it was the predilection of the Judges in favour of the Common Law; for they soon relinquished their Equity Jurisdiction: one reason for which is probably mentioned by Sir Elijah Impey himself, in the Letter quoted in the Introduction. Vide Ante.

The general principles of equity and natural justice are the same in all countries; but when they come to be modified by local circumstances, and a thousand other accidental differences; and when the knowledge of these differences is made a study and a profession *, I really question whether a professional man be not the most unfit of all persons to be transplanted to another country, to administer justice there. Lawyers have been metaphorically stiled " High Priests of the Temple of Justice;" but I believe nobody would ever think of recommending a person who professed one mode of faith, to be the high priest of a distant nation who professed a different mode,

* A celebrated Author observes, " that parts of the " judicial procedure which were at first only accidental, " come in time to be considered as essential; and forma-" lities are accumulated upon each other, till the art of " litigation requires more study than the discovery of " right." The concluding words probably refer to the following passage of Cicero: " Non tam *justitiæ* quam *litigandi vias tradunt.*"

Mr. Justice Blackstone, in his justly admired eulogium on the study of the Law, calls it " a science which em-" ploys, in its theory, the noblest faculties of the soul, " and exerts, in its practice, the cardinal virtues of the " heart." I am afraid the natives of Bengal have not yet discovered the cardinal virtues of the heart, which the practice of the law is said to call forth, unless it be the cardinal virtue of PATIENCE in those who have suffered by it.

though

though both might derive their tenets from the same general code of religious doctrines.

We see even Sir Elijah Impey is obliged, on his first admission to his new office, to renounce one of his most popular, and justly favourite opinions. Some time after his arrival at Calcutta, he established offices for the suits of paupers; and in 1779, we have his own loud applauses of this measure. " Most of the cases
" which we have sent to England," (says he)
" have been brought to light by means of
" these offices for the benefit of paupers; for
" the oppressions of this country have been in
" general so complete, that they have seldom
" left means to the oppressed (if they have not
" met with encouragement or assistance) to
" obtain justice."—Letter to Lord Weymouth, Select Committee's Report, General Appendix, No. 31.

Now let us compare this humane and benevolent Institution, of offices for the suits of paupers, with the following recent regulations of the Provincial Courts of Adaulut*, subject

* These Regulations are printed in the Appendix to the Select Committee's last Report.

to which he has expressly undertaken the office of Judge of the SUDDER ADAULUT.

20. "That if the parties should be found guilty, as is often the case, from litigiousness and perverseness of flying from one Court to another, in order to prevent and protract the course of justice, the party so transgressing shall be considered as non-suited, and according to his degree in life, and the notoriety of the offence, be liable to FINE, IMPRISONMENT, or CORPORAL PUNISHMENT."

21. "That as cases may occur, in which it will be highly necessary, for the welfare of the Crush, to restrain trivial and groundless complaints, and to deter chicane and intrigue, *which passions among the people often work to the undoing of their neighbours*, a discretion shall, in such cases, be left to the Superintendant, either to impose a fine, not exceeding Five Rupees, or inflict a CORPORAL PUNISHMENT, NOT EXCEEDING TWENTY LASHES WITH A RATTAN, according to the degree of the offence, and the person's situation in life." After this, I trust we shall hear no more of the peculiar qualifications of an English Judge for the office of Superintendant of the Sudder Adaulut.

X. I

X. I shall presume to offer one observation more, and it is particularly addressed to the attention of the Legislature. In the years 1772 and 1773, it is well known the affairs of India engaged, and almost engrossed, the whole attention of Parliament. With infinite pains they raised a superstructure, which was to convince the Eastern world of our talents for the office of Legislation, and to remain a lasting monument of our ability, not only to conquer, but to govern the world.—*Hæ tibi erant artes.* —A series of deplorable events has read us a very humiliating lesson on this subject, in the Western world. I am afraid we can take but little occasion to flatter ourselves on the score of political wisdom, from the late transactions of the East.

The result of a two years patient investigation, was the celebrated East India REGULATING-ACT *. The Legislature *conceived*, and brought forth Twins; and the political and judicial parts of that Act were the double offspring of those long and painful throes. The features of both infants were severe, rather than amiable; nor have they, as they advanced in years, much increased in favour with mankind:

" Qui Bavium non odit; amet tua Carmina Mœvi."—

* 13 Geo. III. cap. 63.

It is difficult to say, whether the judicial or the political parts of that system, whether the Court or the Council have most disturbed the peace of India, by their internal divisions, or external opposition.

If there was one point more anxiously provided for in the balance of these two powers than the rest, it was the independence of the Judges, that they might be rendered equal to the great object of their trust, viz. the correction of abuses committed by British subjects. They had large salaries voted them by Parliament; and a prohibitory Clause annexed, forbidding them to accept any other emolument on any account or any pretence whatsoever;— so that we see the Parliament, conscious of the weakness of human nature, and, as if taught by the frailty of its own Members (which *now and then* will appear in the most uncorrupt Assembly), seems to have industriously precluded the influence of Hope in the breasts of the Judges, even if they were disposed to become subservient to the will of the Governor and Council; as well as the operation of Fear, by vesting in the Crown, and not in the Governor and Council, the power of removing them.

That this was the intention of Parliament, I cannot have a doubt; but that this intention was not expressed in sufficient words, I can as little doubt; since two of the greatest lawyers in the kingdom* have declared the appointment

* The following is a pleasant instance of what some wicked wits have called *the glorious uncertainty of the law*. The Court of Directors, wishing to be informed of the legality of this appointment, consulted four of the most eminent Counsel, learned in the laws of England, on the construction of a great legislative Regulation for the government of their possessions in India. The question is no less than, whether the Judges of a Court of Justice, appointed to controul the Governor and Council, and other British subjects in power, may or may not accept great confidential Posts, with large Salaries (that are more likely to increase †, than be diminished), to be held during the pleasure of that very Governor and Council? Two learned Gentlemen (his Majesty's Attorney-General, and Mr. Dunning) answer in the affirmative; two other learned Gentlemen (his Majesty's Solicitor-General, and Mr. Rous) answer in the negative. The former, I presume, admitted that Sir Elijah Impey *could not* receive any other emolument than his 8000l. a year, as Chief Justice; but they thought the very same Sir Elijah Impey *might* legally receive 8000l. a year more, as Judge of the Sudder Adaulut. The latter contended, that the acceptance of the additional 8000l. was contrary both to the spirit and intention of the Legislature; and one of them doubts whether it be not contrary to the words; and the other expressly considers it as a contemptible evasion of the intention of the Legislature. What are the Directors to think, say, or do, on this occasion? Are they to remain

† Information has been received, that an *additional* 6000l. a year, and upwards, has been lately voted for contingent charges. Select Committee's last Report, p. 25.

ment of Sir Elijah Impey to his new office, with a large salary, neither contrary to that statute, nor incompatible with his duty as Chief Justice.

It appears that the legislature, on a supposition that the independence of the Judges was sufficiently secured, intrusted them with very high powers, that can be justified on no other principle. For all future regulations made by the Governor and Council, are to be first registered by the Supreme Court of Judicature, before they become binding.——The legislature conceived, that any regulation which these two bodies (appointed *diverso intuitu*, and established as mutual checks) should concur in, would probably be wise in its principle, and mature in its form.

What is now become of this jealous precaution of the legislature? What is become of this balance adjusted with so much nicety, or of what possible benefit can it

as suspended between these two opinions, thus drawing with equal force, like *Mahomet's Coffin*, between Earth and Heaven? Have they any balance to ascertain their comparative weight? Or shall we advise them to consult four learned Counsellors more; though four more learned Counsellors they will not easily find?——

be

be to uphold this Court, now the public grounds of inſtituting it have ceaſed *.——— When the Houſe of Commons in the laſt century (to compare ſmall things with great) voted the Houſe of Lords "uſeleſs," it was becauſe they feared its oppoſition. If they could have won over that Houſe to an implicit obedience to their meaſures, all mankind would have *concurred,* in declaring it to be " uſeleſs."

I will not diſhonour the Chief Juſtice or the Governor, by ſuppoſing that the one would impoſe, or the other execute, any arbitrary mandate, that might require ſuch ſort of ſacrifices of reputation and conſcience on the part of the Chief Juſtice, as the writer of a pamphlet, I have already quoted, too plainly inſinuates †. ———But it has been often obſerved, that laws are made to guard againſt what men *may* do; not to truſt to what they *will* do. As a public meaſure, therefore, to be vindicated on public

* We may aſk with Dr. Tucker, *Cui bono?*

† " By a little management, *all* the Judges,—ſome of " them certainly, may be gained, and influenced to be " paſſive at leaſt, if not to do whatever they are bid, in " any queſtion that touches the intereſt or authority of " the government; or where it may be the *object of a* " *prevailing party in the Council to run down and ruin an* " *obnoxious individual.*" Extract from an Original Letter from Calcutta.

grounds, we have a right to presume, that power ill obtained will be ill applied; and it is then natural to inquire, where is there any check or controul at hand *?

It ought to be mentioned, that some little trial of the principles of this compromise, between the Council and the Court, has been already made. A tax was lately imposed by an ordinance of the Governor and Council on the inhabitants of Calcutta (both British and natives), for the useful purpose of improving that city, and regulating the police. As the tax, though laudable in its object, was somewhat severe in its *quantum*, it excited considerable opposition; I have been informed, that petitions were presented to the Supreme Court, to prevent this ordinance from being registered. Had the Judges refused their assent, it might have given them a moment's popularity in India; And (such is the fluctuation of public

---

* The objections to the appointment in this light, are summed up with irresistible weight by the highest Authority, next to a positive declaration of the House of Commons; I mean by the Select Committee in their late Report. I know not how far it may be regular, to refer to their observations; but strong reasoning, expressed in the most forcible language, are or ought to be materials *publici Juris*, wherever they occur, either in or out of Parliament.

opinion)

opinion) might, for ought I know, have entirely done away all thofe fentiments of difguft and deteftation, which their former conduct excited.—The tax however paffed, and one of the Judges (Sir Robert Chambers) is placed at the head of a new commiffion of police; but I believe without any falary.

It is the nature and policy of all power, while it is yet unfledged, to make fhort excurfions, and to approach by gentle gradations. Let us fuppofe, in the cafe of fome *future* Governor, and fome *future* Chief Juftice, an obnoxious and profligate meafure fhould be brought forward! who are to oppofe it? not the natives; " it is their peculiar temper (fays Sir Elijah) " to expect every thing from power, and little " from juftice *."——Not the Britifh fubjects,
for

* This is a part of a letter to the Governor and Council, refpecting fome applications that NUNDECOMAR had made, pending his imprifonment and trial. The whole paffage is worth notice, as it will fhew Sir Elijah Impey's opinions *at that time*, which was five years before he accepted the office of fuperintendent of the Sudder Adaulut, revocable at the pleafure of the Governor and Council. " Should he (Nundecomar) continue to addrefs himfelf to " the board; that which will, and can only, be obtained " from principles of juftice, may have the appearance of " being obtained by the means of influence and autho- " rity. The peculiar turn of mind of the natives being

for they are jointly under the controul of the Governor and Chief Justice, without a jury in civil suits, and without any check in political emergencies.

To apply the former instance, the power of TAXATION is one of the highest powers that a government can exercise. I know not why the same authority, which might tax British Subjects at Calcutta, for any purpose however salutary, might not extend through the whole provinces of Bengal, Bahar, and Orissa, for all purposes. Without the assent of the Supreme Court, I believe no person will contend, that the Governor and Council of Bengal can impose a tax on British Subjects. Does the assent of a Court of Justice appointed by the King, *legalize* such an exertion of power? I leave the argument to the consideration of those who claim to be the sole disposers of the PURSE of the SUBJECT. I only mention it as a further reason, for preserving the Judges of the Supreme Court, free from every the remotest influence of the Governor and Council.

" *to expect every thing from power, and little from justice.*
" I know I shall be pardoned the observation, being
" clearly convinced, that the Board would be as cautious
" in furnishing ground for, *as the Judges can be jealous of*
" *incurring*, the imputation." Select Comm. Rep. No. 3. References.

I have

I have now brought the History of the Supreme Court down to the period of the latest dispatches from Bengal, and have stated what, I believe (without being accused of begging the question), I may call some of the grievances that have been felt from the institution of this Court. What remedy these various inconveniences may admit, is a subject of great nicety and difficulty. I have found it a much easier task to describe the symptoms of disorder, than I should to prescribe the cure.—If one of the first Political Characters of this country, in treating of a subject upon which the whole range of his great mind had long been exercised (the reformation of the Civil Government): If even he, was obliged to confess, that " he ap-
" proached it with that awe and reverence
" with which a young physician approaches to
" the cure of the disorders of his parent*;"—
I may surely make an honourable retreat, without attempting to offer a remedy to the disorders I have already described.——

* Speech of Edmund Burke, Esq. on presenting to the House of Commons a plan for the better security of the independence of Parliament, and the œconomical reformation of the Civil and other Establishments. Printed for Dodsley, 1780.

It may argue the unskilfulness of a young Practitioner; but I confess, that like DOCTOR LAST, I see no remedy short of a *radical* cure. It will cost more Lacks of Rupees to the East India Company to patch up the old system, than to send out a new* Court of Justice on a simpler

---

* It has been proposed to appoint a single Judge, with a deputy to assist him, similar to the Chancellor and the Master of the Rolls in England. The Superior Judge to be confined to causes exceeding 200l. in value, except they are tried by consent before the inferior, from whom an appeal might lie to the Superior Judge in all cases exceeding one hundred pounds.

The revival of the Mayor's Court with some alterations and extension of its powers, the Mayor and Aldermen to be chosen by the principal householders (natives and British) in Calcutta, and not to be removeable by the Governor and Council, has likewise been recommended, and I believe would be a very popular institution. An able Recorder acquainted with the laws of England, would in such case be necessary to assist their judgment in points of difficulty.

The probable difference of expence between either of these Courts, properly constituted, and the present Court, would be an immense saving to the Company. The Old Mayor's Court, for the five years preceding its abolition, cost the Company only about 9000l. The Supreme Court, in about the same space of time, has stood the Company in, as appears from the charges actually upon their books, upwards of 360,000l. sterling. And these charges Mr. HASTINGS observes, in one of his minutes, dated March 9, 1780, " Though they may be a fair and accurate state
" of all the expence and losses which stand on the books
" of

plan. As long as the present Judges continue, every new regulation will be " the fruitful " mother" of new offices and new appointments, and all this, I am afraid, must be quietly submitted to, if the Governor and Council are expected to fulfil their other numerous and complicated duties *.

There

" of the Company, will convey but a very inadequate idea
" of the loss which these Provinces have sustained by the
" institution of this Court; a loss which must ultimately
" fall upon the Company; nor of that which the Company
" hath suffered in the first instance by impediments and
" discouragements, thrown in the way of the Collectors
" of the Revenues, of which the representations on our
" Records from the Provincial Councils and Collectors
" afford numberless instances; or by the spirit of contu-
" macy and resistance excited in the *Zemindars* and Farm-
" ers of the Revenue; or by a total stop being put to the
" administration of justice in the Country Courts, which
" compels the natives of all orders, who are possessed of
" sufficient means to resort to *Calcutta* from the most dis-
" tant parts of the country, where, from their ignorance
" of our laws and customs, they are left wholly to the
" mercy of Attornies and practitioners of the Court: while
" the body of the people, who have not property to carry
" on a law-suit, remain in a state of anarchy, without pro-
" tection, or the means of obtaining redress."

* Mr. Hastings has given a lively and animated description of the duties and occupations of a Governor of Bengal, in a letter addressed to the Court of Directors in 1773, (long before the disputes with the Supreme Court were added to the other embarrassments of the State). ' I dare appeal' (says he) ' to the public Records, to

' the

There is one point, however, which I cannot help seriously recommending to those, to whose Province it will fall to correct the present system of judicature; and that is, whether they will, in any case whatever, suffer a native TO BE SUED in the English Court? Let the Supreme Court (if it *must* subsist) be open to natives of every description, to prefer their complaints against the oppression of Europeans;—let the

' the testimony of those who have an opportunity of
' knowing me, and even to the detail which the public
' voice can repeat of the past acts of this government,
' that my time has been neither idly nor uselessly em-
' ployed. Yet such are the cares and embarrassments of
' this various State, that although much be done, much
' more even in the matters of moment must remain ne-
' glected. To select from the miscellaneous heap which
' each day's exigencies present to our choice, those points
' on which the general welfare of your affairs most essen-
' tially depends, to provide expedients for future advan-
' tages, and guard against probable evils, are all that
' your administration can faithfully promise to perform
' for your service, with their united labours most diligently
' exerted.

' The extent of Bengal, and its possible resources, are
' equal to those of most States in Europe. Its difficulties are
' greater than those of any, because it wants both an esta-
' blished form and powers of government; deriving its
' actual support from the unremitted labours and personal
' exertions of individuals in power, instead of the vital in-
' fluence which flows though the channels of a regular
' constitution, and imperceptibly animates every part of
' it.' ————

present Judges of this Court (if they have shewn themselves worthy of so great a trust) continue to decide these suits without a jury; let the British subject (if it be thought necessary to fix so severe a stigma on our countrymen in India) find himself stript of his native right to a trial by his Peers *, the moment he sets foot in that country; let him be pu-

---

* I believe so harsh and unconstitutional a measure as disfranchising a large body of British subjects (for such the depriving them of a trial by jury is in effect), for the purpose of bestowing an ideal or speculative good upon another body of men (the native-suitors in the Supreme Court), cannot be vindicated on any principles of our government or laws.

Upon a presumption of general delinquency, and upon prejudices unsustained by any legal proof, many hundred British subjects are pronounced incapable of exercising impartially the functions of jurymen. Is this Law, or is it Justice? Or was it done to gratify a certain fondness for what Mr. Justice Blackstone calls "New and arbitrary "methods of trial, which, under a variety of plausible pre- "tences, may in time imperceptibly undermine this best "preservative of English Liberty."——And is this unconstitutional innovation to be kept on foot, for fear of mortifying the private feelings of the present Judges in Bengal! It does not appear that the mode of trial which is substituted in the room of trial by Jury, is any *benefit* to the natives, but is only ten times more tedious and expensive; and a petty cause, which would be decided by a sensible jury in an hour or two, is by the absurdities of taking written depositions, and of translating and retranslating them, and the blunders of the Clerks in Court, two or three days in determining!

nishable

nishable in his person and fortune (as by law he is) for the acts of such natives as he employs, and as *bonâ fide* his agents :——but do not, under colour of protecting the native from the oppressions of other natives, introduce uncertain standards, and vague statute definitions, which in their legal consequences may extend to make every native of rank, character, and opulence in the Provinces, liable to be sued in that Court; and to be suddenly dragged away to a distant Judicature, at the instigation of private malice; to be thrown into the Calcutta prison for want of bail*; to be compelled to prove, that he is not within the construction of an English Statute; and if he succeeds in establishing, to the satisfaction of the Judges (zealous like all other Judges to enlarge the circle of their authority), that he is not within the jurisdiction, that is, to *prove a negative*,—to be at last turned adrift at Calcutta, far from his native home, without money, and without friends, his reputation sullied, his credit ruined, and the only satisfaction left him is to bring an action in the same Supreme Court

---

* There is but one Sheriff for the immensely populous, and extensive Provinces of Bengal, Bahar, and Orissa: Whereas in England and Wales, with not half the number of inhabitants, we have at least *fifty-two* Sheriffs, authorised to take bail, besides a number of subordinate judicatures throughout the country.

against

against his opponent, for maliciously causing him to be arrested.——Is this redress? or is it not a mockery to his feelings *?

If the remarks I have presumed to offer in the introduction be founded either on law or common sense, or (what is above both) on experience; no possible form of words can be framed to include native agents within the jurisdiction which will not become the basis of successive interpretations, and, like a Speaking Trumpet, be made to convey any sense the Judges please. No words appear at first sight a less exceptionable description of such natives as might be supposed to be agents of British Subjects, than " persons directly or indirectly " in their service or employment, or in the " service and employment of the Company:" And yet we see that these words, in their necessary operation and constructive extension, have been successively enlarged till this new jurisdiction became as unbounded in fact, as the most comprehensive words could have made it.——And in the Bill that was brought into

---

* That this account is not exaggerated, vid. innumerable instances in the representations of the Governor and Council.——These evils are in truth inherent in the constitution of a Court, which, though limited as to the objects of its jurisdiction, is Supreme in its authority, and claims a right of summoning every native, and making him *prove* his exemption, before he can be discharged.

Parliament the laſt ſeſſion, it required upwards of ſixty ſections or ſeparate clauſes to correct the miſchief that had been produced by theſe few vague words,——" directly or " indirectly, &c."

It has been ingeniouſly argued, that the extenſion of this judicature never can happen without the co-operation of the natives; and that if they are the objects, they are likewiſe the *Inſtruments* of this extenſion. There can be no ſuit without ſuitors; and the plaintiff at leaſt approves the juriſdiction, when he repairs to it for juſtice. So far indeed it is true, as Mr. Barwell ſtates, that ' many Zemindars
' and others, who complained of the opera-
' tion of the juriſdiction upon them, and were
' anxious to be exempted, yet applied to the
' Court in purſuit of redreſs, or to ſcreen
' themſelves under ſome proceſs of law,
' againſt either the acts of government in
' inforcing payment of its rents, or of in-
' dividuals proſecuting in the Country
' Courts of Juſtice.' Select Com. Rep. p. 58. But I do not believe it will furniſh any very powerful argument for the extenſion of this judicature, by ſhewing, that it produces a defalcation of the Company's revenues, or that it gratifies litigious paſſions.——From the beſt
informa-

information that can be collected, it appears, the natives in Calcutta would never resort to the Supreme Court but for the purpose of private revenge. The distinction of CASTS throughout Hindostan is well-known to create a difference of rank, which, more than opulence or power, raises one native above another. It is a high gratification to a worthless man of a vindictive disposition, to be able to punish a man of a superior CAST[*], This he effects by threatening him with an action in the Supreme Court, whether he has grounds or not: for he knows he disgraces his adversary, by making him appear in an English Court; and many instances might be cited of family being set in array against family, and the peace and quiet of domestic life being cruelly invaded, by the easy means of gratifying a momentary resentment, which the Supreme Court affords.

[*] Vid. Sir Elijah Impey's Letters before quoted, vide p. 23. Introd. Notes. Hindoos of a high Cast, he says, and Mussulmen of high rank, think it so great a disgrace to take an oath, that they will rather stand out the utmost rigour of the laws: and " they would pay any demand " sooner than answer an oath to a bill of equity." A woman Hindoo, or Moor, if not the outcast of the people, can by no process be compelled to make her personal appearance in a Court of Justice. An accusation against her, if she must be brought forth to make answer, is equal to a sentence of capital punishment. Vid. Rep. Sel. Com. *passim.*

But

But it is not for the vindictive, or even discontented and querulous suitor, that we ought to feel on such occasions, it is for the quiet, mild, and gentle Indian, who wishes to conform to the institutions of his fathers, and has no idea, that by living according to the institutions of his country, he offends against a foreign law, or that he is every hour exposed to have his conduct tried by an unknown rule of action, which may affix ideas of criminality and guilt to acts that are perfectly innocent, or indifferent, by the laws of his native country. I must insist upon this more fully, because the jurisdiction of the Supreme Court is countenanced (nay expressly confirmed) by the Act of last Session in and throughout the populous city of Calcutta; that is, over a body of natives amounting to between FOUR OR FIVE HUNDRED THOUSAND*, not above one thousand

---

* The Act of last Session leaves the *criminal* law of England as it found it, to operate in full force upon these natives: So that, according to the objection of the Court of Directors, in their Memorial before cited, any native may still be prosecuted, like Nundecomar, for capital offences against our laws, when the like offences may be penal in a much inferior degree by his own. And " every " man" (to adopt one of their instances) " convicted for " the first time of bigamy, which is allowed, protected, " and almost commanded by their law, be burnt in the " hand if he can read, and hanged if he cannot read."— Here, however, the Court of Directors have made a small mistake

fand of whom (upon the moſt enlarged computation) underſtand our language, and ſtill leſs our laws. I much doubt, whether this affirmance, of what was before a doubtful juriſdiction, be ſufficiently guarded, by enacting, that ſuch ſuits ſhall be determined by the laws of the Mahomedans or Gentoos reſpectively; (as the parties ſhall be), becauſe it is really impoſſible for Engliſh Judges not to have a ſtrong bias in favour of their own laws which they know, and in which they are bred; and a natural prejudice againſt Mahomedan and Gentoo laws, with which they are unacquainted. Beſides, it is ſurely repoſing too much confidence in the preſent Judges; and is exacting from minds, that are known to be ſtrongly prejudiced, a degree of liberality that can hardly be expected from the moſt enlarged underſtandings and unbiaſſed integrity.

miſtake in point of law. The criterion of *reading*, in order to entitle a convict to the benefit of Clergy, is aboliſhed by a Statute of Queen Ann. It was doubted, before that Statute, whether Jews, Infidels, or other Heretics, could be entitled to their benefit of Clergy, as they could never have taken Orders in Holy Church. According to this diſtinction (which however is certainly not law), a Mahomedan or a Gentoo muſt loſe the benefit of Clergy, becauſe incapable of entering into Holy Orders. This is another precious abſurdity, of attempting to apply our laws to the natives of India! were not the ridicule loſt in the national diſgrace and folly of the attempt!

The

The temporary Act, that was passed last Session (after enumerating various classes of natives who shall not be within the jurisdiction of the Court), endeavours to bring back the Supreme Court to the real principles on which it was instituted, by declaring, that such natives as *are* within the jurisdiction, shall not be answerable there " for matters of inheritance " or succession, or matters of dealing or con- " tract, except for actions of wrongs or tres- " passes *." But though that Act has pared away a considerable portion of the Court's acquired jurisdiction, it has given it a jurisdiction, in other respects, which is not only sufficiently ample, but which, it is to be apprehended, will revive new constructions, not less pernicious than the former; and the natural question then is,

" What boots it at one gate to make defence,
" And at another to let in the foe?"

* What the Supreme Court will choose to call *wrongs* or *trespasses*, I believe no lawyer in this country can predict. Any Act of authority, attended with coercion, is a *trespass*, unless it be strictly justified by the technical rules of law; and the native will be hampered in all the nets of special-pleading, before he can come to the merits of the case. As to the legal definition of *wrongs*, it is a word of still greater latitude.

I will

I will venture to prophefy, that, with a twentieth part of the ingenuity the prefent Judges have fhewn, the late Act of the Britifh Parliament will prove as feeble a barrier againft the extenfion of their jurifdiction, as an ordinance of the Great Mogul, or his " man of " ftraw *," the prefent Nabob of Bengal.

As the jurifdiction is limited by the Act of laft year, natives of the following defcription are ftill amenable to the Supreme Court:

ALL NATIVES, " employed by the Company, or " the Governor General and Council, or by any per- " fon deriving authority under them, or by any na- " tive, or defcendant of a native of Great Britain †," in actions for wrongs or trefpaffes.

ALL NATIVE MAGISTRATES, for any corrupt act or acts.

ALL NATIVES refident at Calcutta, as has been juft mentioned ‡.

Confident

---

* So called by one of the Judges on the Bench.

† Thefe general expreffions were introduced to *correct* the latitude of the former Statute, viz. *directly or indirectly in the fervice of Britifh Subjects or the Company.* Qu. As to their probable operation in the Supreme Court?

‡ There are feveral claufes in this Act (which were left ftanding in the Houfe of Lords, when fo many valuable parts of the elaborate and extenfive Bill that was originally framed, were cut away) that appear to me to contain new materials

Confident as I am that the benefit of allowing any natives, of what description soever, to be

materials of uncertainty and dispute; I mean those clauses, which, *for the more perfectly ascertaining such natives as are amenable to the Supreme Court*, order all natives, employed by British Subjects, as stewards, agents, or partners in matters of revenue or merchandize, to be *registered*; and inflict divers penalties and forfeitures for neglecting so to do.—On these clauses, the following observations occur:

1. It is made highly penal in a British Subject to neglect registering his native agent; at the same time the Act affords no clue to interpret what constitutes an agent in a matter of revenue or merchandize. Does it mean every person employed in the lowest offices of a warehouse, manufactory, &c. or only Gomastahs and Banyans? Are the servants of a Collector of Revenue, and to what extent, and in what degree, within these words?

2. They are said to be, for more clearly ascertaining what *natives* are subject, &c.; yet it does not appear that such register is made conclusive evidence, or any evidence at all, so as to affect the native in a plea to the jurisdiction of the Supreme Court.

3. The British Subject is left in the dark to pronounce what an agent means; and the penalty of 500 l. on every case of omission, attaches upon the Supreme Court's construction of a doubtful term. In the 13th Geo. III. we have the *description* of an agent; in the 21st Geo. III. we have the *term* itself. The description cost upwards of sixty clauses to explain it. Will the difficulty be cured by substituting the term for the definition? Will not this be setting the two Acts of Parliament to run in a circle? *et se sequiturque fugitque.*

4. If

be fued in the Supreme Court, will be infinitely outweighed by the hardships and inconveniences of subjecting them to our laws, which in their principles are so repugnant to their own, and in their forms of process are so tedious, expensive, and complicated, I cannot help recommending, that this Court be inhibited from holding any plea whatever, BETWEEN NATIVE AND NATIVE. The Chief Justice himself asserts, that if the Court were to sit only on causes between the

4. If a British Subject omits to register his native in any concern of revenue or merchandize, he forfeits 500 l. and all the profits. Now, for certain British Subjects, in the Company's Service, to engage in trade at all, is severely reprehended and forbidden by 13 Geo. III. which continues unrepealed; so that omitting to register an agent in an illegal transaction, is declared doubly illegal. This is what may be called a *cumulative* law, in a new sense! If you engage in trade it is penal; if you do not proclaim it to the world, it is penal in a still higher degree.

5. But the unfortunate native is reduced to a worse dilemma. If his master, or partner, or employer, omits to register his name, he loses not only his salary, but all his profits; and whoever sues for the same shall be entitled to recover. Thus, for the omission of a formality, of which the native is ignorant, he forfeits his salary and profits (the labour of years perhaps), and is obliged to refund all that he has actually received for ever so long a time!

These appear to me strong objections against those clauses. I offer them with the greatest deference and respect to the consideration of those who are much better judges than myself, how far they deserve a revision, or a total expulsion from the Act.

Black

Black Inhabitants of Calcutta, they could not go through with one half of them; and I refer to his own forcible reprefentations, in the year 1775, of the manifold impediments to the ordinary adminiftration of juftice in the Supreme Court, from circumftances that " have their " fource (as he ftates it) in the religion, man- " ners, and prejudices of the natives *."

If the hazardous idea of eftablifhing an Englifh Judicature, to which natives are to be fued, ftill predominates, I only wifh the words of Mr. BARWELL † may have their due weight. They are full of intrinfic good fenfe; and he can be fufpected of no bias againft the Supreme Court. This Gentleman being afked his opinion, refpecting the probable benefit the natives would derive from the inftitution of Circuits, and the eftablifhment of more Courts of Judicature, fimilar to, and fubordinate to, the Supreme Court; anfwered, That ' any In- ' ftitution, which may be formed upon the

---

* General Appendix, Select Committee's Report, No. 31.—A better refutation cannot be conceived of the Chief Juftice's claims and affertions in the year 1780, than his own Letters in 1775.

† I quote Mr. BARWELL's evidence in preference, becaufe he is known to be politically and perfonally a friend to the Chief Juftice; and if he is not a friend to the Supreme Court, it can only flow from conviction.

' practice

'practice of our Courts, will make the whole system so exceedingly complicated, so novel, and so little suited to the genius of the people, that he believes it would multiply the evils that are already experienced. A summary and more simple mode of administring justice, is the only Institution which can be beneficial to a country, the majority of the inhabitants of which support themselves and families upon so trifling an income as 3 *l.* 10 *s. per annum.*"—Select Committee's Report, page 57.

I repeat it again: Let Europeans of every description be amenable to the Supreme Court; let them be answerable for their own acts, and for those of their agents; but do not, for the sake of including their native-agents within the jurisdiction, and indulging an illusory hope of benefits, that never will be realized, set up an indeterminate rule, which must revive the former mischiefs, and lead through the same mazes to the same termination; or perhaps, by opening a new door to questions of a disputed jurisdiction, let in a multitude of fresh evils, heavier than the former. If it be said the Court will be of no use, unless natives of a certain description are made amenable; I answer, that the object which the Legislature ought to have in view, on this and every occasion,

casion, is to produce the greatest possible good, at the risque of the least possible mischief; but if the benefit to be expected is more than over-balanced by the probable evil to be dreaded, the whole system is radically defective. Of this kind, I contend, is the jurisdiction of the Supreme Court over the natives of India.—Either exclude it from this jurisdiction by a sound general law; or, if the expence of the Court be too grievous to be borne on the single condition of its "doing no mischief," the other branch of the alternative is obvious,—abolish it.—It is a part of political wisdom to anticipate Necessity, and

"To do that early, we must do at last."

FINIS.

www.ingramcontent.com/pod-product-compliance
Lightning Source LLC
Chambersburg PA
CBHW020304170426
43202CB00008B/498